# Effective Practice Learning in Social Work

**Transforming Social Work Practice – titles in the series**

| | |
|---|---|
| Applied Psychology for Social Work | TBC |
| Collaborative Social Work Practice | ISBN-10: 1 84445 014 7<br>ISBN-13: 978 1 84445 014 5 |
| Communication and Interpersonal Skills in Social Work | ISBN-10: 1 84445 019 8<br>ISBN-13: 978 1 84445 019 0 |
| Effective Practice Learning in Social Work | ISBN-10: 1 84445 015 5<br>ISBN-13: 978 1 84445 015 2 |
| Management and Organisations in Social Work | ISBN-10: 1 84445 044 9<br>ISBN-13: 978 1 84445 044 2 |
| Social Work and Human Development | ISBN-10: 1 90330 083 5<br>ISBN-13: 978 1 90330 083 1 |
| Social Work and Mental Health  (second edition) | ISBN-10: 1 84445 068 6<br>ISBN-13: 978 1 84445 068 8 |
| Social Work in Education and Children's Services | ISBN-10: 1 84445 045 7<br>ISBN-13: 978 1 84445  045 9 |
| Social Work Practice: Assessment, Planning, Intervention and Review | ISBN-10: 1 90330 085 1<br>ISBN-13: 978 1 90330 085 5 |
| Social Work with Children and Families | ISBN-10: 1 84445 018 X<br>ISBN-13: 978 1 84445 018 3 |
| Social Work with Children, Young People and their Families in Scotland | ISBN-10: 1 84445 031 7<br>ISBN-13: 978 1 84445 031 2 |
| Social Work with Drug and Substance Misusers | ISBN-10: 1 84445 058 9<br>ISBN-13: 978 1 84445 058 9 |
| Social Work with Older People | ISBN-10:  1 84445 017 1<br>ISBN-13: 978 1 84445 017 6 |
| Social Work with People with Learning Difficulties | ISBN-10: 1 84445 042 2<br>ISBN-13: 978 1 84445 042 8 |
| Using the Law in Social Work (second edition) | ISBN-10: 1 84445 030 9<br>ISBN-13: 978 1 84445 030 5 |
| Values and Ethics in Social Work | ISBN-10: 1 84445 067 8<br>ISBN-13: 978 1 84445 067 1 |
| What is Social Work? Context and Perspectives (second edition) | ISBN-10: 1 84445 055 1<br>ISBN-13: 978 1 84445 055 1 |
| Youth Justice and Social Work | ISBN-10: 1 84445 066 X<br>ISBN-13: 978 1 84445 066 4 |

To order, please contact our distributor: BEBC Distribution, Albion Close, Parkstone, Poole, BH12 3LL. Telephone: 0845 230 9000, email: learningmatters@bebc.co.uk. You can also find more information on each of these titles and our other learning resources at www.learningmatters.co.uk.

# Effective Practice Learning in Social Work

## JONATHAN PARKER

Series Editors: Jonathan Parker and Greta Bradley

LearningMatters

First published in 2004 by Learning Matters Ltd.

Reprinted twice in 2005
Reprinted in 2006

*British Library Cataloguing in Publication Data*
A CIP record for this book is available from the British Library.

ISBN-10: 1 84445 015 5
ISBN-13: 978 1 84445 015 2

Cover and text design by Code 5 Design Associates Ltd
Project management by Deer Park Productions
Typeset by Pantek Arts Ltd, Maidstone, Kent
Printed and bound in Great Britain by Bell & Bain Ltd, Glasgow

Learning Matters Ltd
33 Southernhay East
Exeter EX1 1NX
Tel: 01392 215560
info@learningmatters.co.uk
www.learningmatters.co.uk

# Contents

## Acknowledgements

I would like to thank the social work teams, the practice teachers and social work students I have worked with over the years who have made this book possible.

I must also extend my thanks to Barbara, for her patience and forbearance whilst writing.

# Introduction

The new honours degree level qualification for social work practice emphasises the centrality of learning for and in practice and learning to practise. Indeed, the Department of Health requirements for the degree state clearly that all students must undertake at least 200 days in direct practice learning during their programme of study. These 200 days must be taken in at least two separate practice agencies and include experience of working with two different service user groups.

Two hundred days spent in practice learning represents a major proportion of your study time on the programme and the importance of the practice learning experience cannot be underestimated for social work students, their practice teachers/assessors, the agencies in which practice is undertaken and the academic staff involved in social work education.

Practice learning tends, however, to raise great anxieties within students, within agencies and within those who facilitate, supervise and assess the practice learning. This book seeks to address some of the complex and anxiety-provoking issues involved in practice learning, to offer an introduction and guide to the process and to seek ways in which student learning can be maximised, using the National Occupational Standards which underpin the assessment of practice learning as a benchmark.

This book is written for student social workers following a qualifying degree programme who are beginning to develop their skills and understanding of the requirements for practice and who are undertaking or about to undertake practice learning. It will also be helpful to student supervisors and practice teachers or assessors and be of interest to trainers and policy-makers within social care agencies and healthcare professions in which practice learning is also undertaken. The book will also appeal to people considering a career in social work or social care but not yet studying for a social work degree as it will introduce you to some of the ways in which social workers practise. It is intended to be used throughout your practice learning experiences depending on how your programme is designed.

## Requirements for social work education

Social work education has undergone a major transformation to ensure that qualified social workers are educated to honours degree level and develop knowledge, skills and values which are common and shared. A vision for social work operating in complex human situations has been adopted. This is reflected in the following definition from the International Association of Schools of Social Work and International Federation of Social Workers (2001):

> *The social work profession promotes social change, problem solving in human relationships and the empowerment and liberation of people to enhance well-being.*

*Utilising theories of human behaviour and social systems, social work intervenes at the points where people interact with their environments. Principles of human rights and social justice are fundamental to social work.*

While there is a great deal packed into this short and pithy definition it encapsulates the notion that social work concerns individual people and wider society. Social workers work with people who are vulnerable, who are struggling in some way to participate fully in society. Social workers walk that tightrope between individuals excluded from taking a place within society and the social and political environment that may have contributed to their marginalisation.

Social workers need to be highly skilled and knowledgeable to work effectively in this context. The Minister of Health is keen for social work education and practice to improve. In order to improve the quality of both these aspects of professional social work, it is crucial that you, as a student social worker, develop high-level skills in practice and in applying theories and models for social work. Such knowledge helps social workers to know what to do, when to do it and how to do it, while recognising that social work is a complex activity with no absolute 'rights' and 'wrongs' of practice for each situation. We also agree with the previous Minister in championing the practical focus of social work, of being able to apply our knowledge to help others.

*Social work is a very practical job. It is about protecting people and changing their lives, not about being able to give a fluent and theoretical explanation of why they got into difficulties in the first place. New degree courses must ensure that theory and research directly informs and supports practice.*

*The Requirements for Social Work Training set out the minimum standards for entry to social work degree courses and for the teaching and assessment that social work students must receive. The new degree will require social workers to demonstrate their practical application of skills and knowledge and their ability to solve problems and provide hope for people relying on social services for support.*

(Jacqui Smith, Minister of Health, 2002)

## Book structure

There are six core chapters to this book. We begin in Chapter 1 by considering the centrality of a strong value base and ethical code for practice. The requirements for practice contained within the GSCC Code of Practice and reinforced by the National Occupational Standards are outlined and you are introduced to the application of anti-oppressive and anti-discriminatory approaches in the practice setting. Key issues affecting your practice learning opportunity are discussed. These include the impact of whistleblowing policies and procedures for ending a student's practice learning. You will be encouraged to reflect on the value base outlined by the social work professional body and critique values and anti-oppressive practice in the workplace.

In Chapter 2 you will examine aspects of integrating theory and practice and consider the role of reflection in promoting integration. A monumental challenge for many students concerns the use of theories, methods and models in practice settings. So often students

– and indeed practitioners – will avoid theories and methods, state that they do not see their relevance or actively renounce them. However, in this chapter theories are seen as guiding actions and providing explanatory frameworks that make effective interventions possible. You will be encouraged to examine some of the barriers to using theories and methods in practice and to seek solutions that can be tested and refined through continual reflection on practice learning. The practical relevance of theory will be emphasised and the Department of Health (2002, p3) requirement to 'ensure that the teaching of theoretical knowledge, skills and values is based on their application in practice' will underpin discussion. In this chapter you will also develop an understanding of reflective practice. This is not an easy concept to grasp but it is central to your learning. You will therefore be introduced to the development of reflection in professional education, together with some models and activities for encouraging reflection during your practice learning.

The new degree in social work includes a requirement for students to be assessed as fit for practice learning and in Chapter 3 we explore a number of ways of becoming prepared and helping to prepare yourself for practice learning. There are many steps you can take yourself to ensure you are ready to maximise gains from the practice learning experience and to give your best to the learning setting and agency. In this chapter, individual issues such as personal learning styles and theories or principles of adult learning will be considered. You will be invited to identify issues in the learning process for yourself that may assist in preparing for practice learning. Your university's processes will be considered and you are encouraged to become actively involved in the matching, selection and negotiation process as far as your home university – and the agency – will allow. There will be a chance to reflect on and identify learning needs and to set an action plan for meeting those needs by examining the use and development of a practice curriculum to structure the experience.

In the fourth chapter, you will be introduced to the important activity of supervision and the purposes for which it is used, especially in respect of encouraging learning. The responsibilities and accountabilities of the supervision process will be examined and you will be taken through a series of activities and reflective exercises to examine what they might do to use the process effectively and maximise the benefits gained from supervision.

Practice learning opportunities are rigorously assessed and we turn to assessment issues in Chapter 5. This demands that you know what is to be assessed and how it will be evaluated. It also requires you to become effective in self-assessment, reflecting on learning, identifying needs and working out learning plans to meet needs within the context of practice. This chapter examines the assessment process and the requirements of the National Occupational Standards to be achieved. We will consider what constitutes evidence, how it can be gathered, displayed and used to demonstrate growing competence. Links will be drawn with the assessment of ethical and anti-oppressive practice as presented in Chapter 1.

Following on from Chapter 5, the final core chapter explores the range of communication skills to be developed to show competent practice. These skills include interpersonal communication between the student and service users and carers, with colleagues in the practice agency and with other professionals and agencies. The skills examined go deeper, however, than interpersonal communication and we will look at ways of communicating effectively using the telephone, by writing letters and in professional reports. An important part of this chapter considers the communication skills needed for compiling and presenting an effective self-evaluation report showing the learning that has taken place, the evidence on which you might judge the practice learning experience and your future learning needs. This includes an examination of what should go into a self-evaluation report and what standards it should be written against.

The book concludes by bringing together the key elements involved in successful practice learning, reviewing the process and promoting ways of developing a continuing approach to learning and development within the practice setting.

# Learning features

The book is interactive. You are encouraged to work through the book as an active participant, taking responsibility for your learning in order to increase your knowledge, understanding and ability to apply this learning to practice. You will be expected to reflect creatively on how immediate learning needs can be met in the areas of assessment, planning, intervention and review and how your professional learning can be developed in your future career.

Case studies throughout the book will help you to examine theories and models for social work practice. We have devised activities that require you to reflect on experiences, situations and events and help you to review and summarise learning undertaken. In this way your knowledge will become deeply embedded as part of your development. When you come to practice learning in an agency the work and reflection undertaken here will help you to improve and hone your skills and knowledge.

This book will introduce knowledge and learning activities for you as a student social worker concerning some of the central processes relating to issues of daily practice in all areas of the discipline. Suggestions for further reading will be made at the end of each chapter.

# Professional development and reflective practice

Great emphasis is placed on developing skills of reflection about, in and on practice. This has developed over many years in social work. It is important also that you reflect prior to practice, as this emphasis on a thoughtful and planned approach will help you make your work clear to service users and also more open to review so you can improve your practice in the future. This book will assist you in developing a questioning approach that looks in a critical way at your thoughts, experiences and practice and seeks to heighten your skills in refining your practice as a result (see especially Chapter 2 but also throughout). Reflection is central to good social work practice, but only if enhanced action results from that reflection.

Reflecting about, in and on your practice is not only important during your practice learning and education to become a social worker, it is considered key to continued professional development. As we move to a profession that acknowledges life-long learning as a way of keeping up to date, ensuring that research informs practice and striving continually to improve skills and values for practice, it is important to begin the process at the outset of your development. The importance of professional development is clearly shown by its inclusion in the National Occupational Standards and is reflected in the GSCC Code of Practice for Employees.

## A note on terminology

Some terms are used interchangeably within the book and they need some clarification. Practice teacher and practice assessor refer to the person responsible for the final recommendation on your practice learning. The two terms, while differences can be found, are used synonymously within the book. This emphasises the teaching and learning aspect of the role and the assessment function. Where it is appropriate to do so a specific function may be added to one of these terms, such as practice teacher-supervisor. This will demonstrate context and role or task to be performed.

The term placement, while still preferred by some, is not used within this book. However, the terms practice learning opportunity or practice learning experience or simply practice learning are used interchangeably to refer to the required learning experience of practising in an agency with service users, carers and others.

# Chapter 1

# Values and anti-oppressive practice in practice learning

**ACHIEVING A SOCIAL WORK DEGREE**

This chapter will help you to meet the following National Occupational Standard:
*Key Role 6: Demonstrate professional competence in social work practice*
- Work within agreed standards of social work practice and ensure own professional development
- Manage complex ethical issues, dilemmas and conflicts
- Contribute to the promotion of best social work practice.

It will also introduce you to the following academic standards as set out in the social work subject benchmark statement:
**3.1.3 Values and ethics**
- Nature, evolution and application of social work values
- Rights, responsibilities, freedom, authority and power in the practice of social workers as moral and statutory agents
- Complex relationship of justice, care and control – practical and ethical implications
- Conceptual links between codes of ethics, regulation of professional conduct and management of potential conflicts generated by codes of different professions
**3.2.2 Problem-solving skills**
- Analyse, take account of the impact of inequality and discrimination
**3.2.4 Skills in working with others**
- Act to increase social justice – identify and respond to discrimination.

## Introduction

This chapter will outline the value requirements for social work and social care practice contained within the GSCC Code of Practice and reinforced by the National Occupational Standards. Attention will be paid to the application of anti-oppressive and anti-discriminatory approaches in the practice setting. Key issues affecting students on placement, including the impact of whistleblowing policies, and procedures for ending students' practice learning will be discussed using clear case examples. Students and practice teachers or assessors using this book will be encouraged to reflect on the value base outlined by the social work professional body, an academic critique of values and anti-oppressive practice and the day-to-day realities of negotiating ethical practice in the workplace as a student.

# Practice learning and social work values

Social work is a value-based activity and can never be neutral. It must be so given that:

> *Social workers deal with some of the most vulnerable people in our society at times of greatest stress. There can be tragic consequences if things go wrong. Social workers often get a bad press. What they do not get is day-to-day coverage of the work they do to protect and provide for some of the most vulnerable people in our society.*

(Smith, Department of Health, 2002, pi)

If you work with people, making decisions that may have far-reaching consequences for their lives, this must be done according to transparent, understandable principles. These requirements may be open to challenge, and often they are. However, in working in an open, up-front way you are demonstrating that you are using values to guide your practice. Values and ethical codes are not always or necessarily 'right', and we cannot claim that social work is based on a set of absolute moral principles. What is important is that these principles for practice promote well-being rather than diminish it, and where they do not, are challenged and revised.

---

**ACTIVITY 1.1**

*Think about your own values and beliefs. What do you believe about people? Are they potentially good or potentially bad? Why is it that you wish to become a social worker and in what ways do you want to make a difference in people's lives? Write down some answers to these questions and consider how your values and beliefs might add to a person's well-being or, perhaps, take it away. These reflections are useful in developing a critical approach to your practice. The process of challenging yourself and continually reviewing what you do, how you do it, why you do it and what implications there might be for yourself and others is a key feature of professional development.*

---

One of the fundamental purposes of practice learning is to ensure that students are safe to practise as social workers, that students learn and are assessed as competent in the practical skills of offering care, support, control and regulation in a supervised environment. This is one of the reasons why the time spent in practice learning has been extended from a minimum of 130 days in the previous qualifying award to at least 200 days in the degree. When you first begin your social work degree, it is common to want to start practising. It is the reason why you have come to study social work and it is not uncommon, initially, for students to feel frustrated at having to wait before starting practice learning (see Chapter 3 for further discussion of preparatory assessment for practice learning). However, not only is it important for social work programme providers to assess you as being safe and 'fit' for practice, but it is also common for students to begin to feel less self-assured and more anxious as the time to begin practice learning approaches. You may question your own readiness to begin, your ability and confidence to put into practice the knowledge, skills and values you have learned within the classroom. You may be anxious that you 'do the right thing' or, at least, do no harm. A degree of anxiety is a good thing. It indicates your readiness to learn from others, to recognise that learning is a continual process, and acknowledges the seriousness of learning to practise. Professional values and ethics in social work education are also important here and social work programmes are committed to educating people as 'fit for purpose and practice'.

While each programme will have a different way of managing, supporting and apportioning days to practice learning, the purpose is clear. It is to assist you to gain and to assess your competence in practising as a social worker. It is, therefore, intimately bound with the values that underpin social work and social care. On your practice learning opportunities you will have access to people who are receiving social work services. As Smith's quotation above notes, people who need social work services are often among some of the most vulnerable in society. For this reason alone it is important to approach your learning in an ethical, reflective and value-based manner to ensure that people are not exploited, manipulated or made more vulnerable by your actions. This means that you will need to reflect honestly on your own thoughts, feelings and prejudices concerning situations and people with whom you come into contact. It also means that you will have to follow closely the stipulations and requirements of your agency, explain these carefully and clearly to the people you are working with and have a growing sense of how people wish to be approached and treated. It is more complex than this, however, and an understanding of social work values is crucial to developing good practice while undertaking practice learning.

## Values, ethics and requirements in social work

### *The question of values*
There is considerable debate about values and ethics in social work. Braye and Preston-Shoot (1995) emphasise that talk about values-based practice permeates every part of social work practice. At times this debate has led to some social workers considering that it is 'values in practice' that define the profession. This does not mean that other professions do not hold clear values. Values and core beliefs may be differently expressed, however, according to the role and tasks of the profession. In an increasingly multi-professional and multi-disciplinary environment in health and social care it is important to learn about the value base of other professions with whom you have contact. By doing so while undertaking practice learning you will be able to better define your own professional identity by recognising difference and diversity and considering the centrality of the values and beliefs underpinning social work.

There is also some debate and a degree of misunderstanding concerning the difference between ethics and values (Clark, 2000). The sense of the terms can become lost or muddled by their overuse. Some of these difficulties stem from the complexity of the terms and concepts used. However, values and ethics have a direct practice bearing on what you will do as a social worker in training during your practice learning and beyond into qualified practice. Clark (2000) is adamant that values and ethics should be distinguished from one another and, wherever possible, defined in ways that promote distinction and understanding.

Professional ethics stem from values but the two terms are not synonymous. A simple understanding is that values concern belief systems that are often personal and internalised while ethics, although they can be adhered to in a similar way, are sets of rules or codes by which a person should practise. However, 'values' is a problematic and complex term that includes economic worth, moral imperatives and 'musts and oughts', culturally adopted behaviours and belief systems. According to Clark (2000), we must be fairly modest and tentative in reaching a definition. He suggests that values:

> *give expression to intuitions and beliefs about the essential ends of human life and social living. Basic values embrace the grand aspirations or big ideas of morality and politics, such as freedom, justice, autonomy and community. Basic values also comprise ideals about the morally good character and the nature of the life worth living, for example compassion, courage, truthfulness or industriousness.*

(Clark, 2000, p28)

Core values in social work are often promoted as lists of principles on which social work practice is based (Horne, 1999). There is a degree of general agreement over principles included within these lists although they differ from author to author to some extent. Clark (2000) suggests that core values in social work concern the dual role of care and control which may be formulated in four key principles:

- the worth and uniqueness of every person;
- the entitlement to justice;
- the aspiration to freedom;
- the essentiality of community.

These principles are encapsulated within a debate about personhood started within dementia care settings but applicable to all areas of social work practice (Kitwood, 1997; Parker, 2001). Kitwood (1997, p8) summarises the essential features of the model of personhood as follows:

> *It is a standing or status that is bestowed upon one human being, by others, in the context of relationship and social being. It implies recognition, respect and trust.*

While there are some complex philosophical arguments surrounding the concept of personhood, it is important to note that it is founded on social relationships and interactions, something that is central to your developing practice.

Values in social work, as sets of principles and beliefs, come from a wide variety of sources as shown in Figure 1.1.

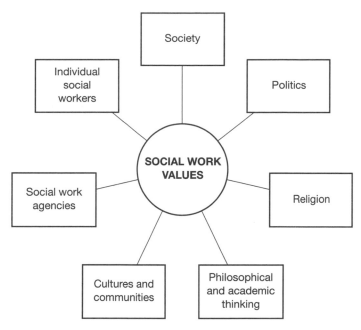

*Figure 1.1* *The sources of social work values*

## Professional ethics and the GSCC Code of Practice

Professional ethics may be more readily defined (Clark, 2000). Codes of ethics for professional practice have two aims: to prescribe how you should deal with a morally problematic or difficult situation in practice, and also to provide a lens through which you may critique and judge the prescriptions that require you to act in that way. Ethics represent rules for practice. They are often produced by professional associations or regulatory bodies but also reflect the standards for practice set and demanded by agencies and government. As Clark (2000, p49) states:

> A 'rule' in this context is a widely accepted, generally binding prescription based on experience and customary practice; but rules are not absolute or infallible, and exceptions have to be allowed occasionally where good reason can be shown.

He identifies eight rules for good social work practice. These comprise:

- respectfulness;
- honesty and truthfulness;
- being knowledgeable and skilful;
- being careful and diligent;
- being effective and helpful;
- ensuring that work is:
  - legitimate and authorised;
  - collaborative and accountable;
  - reputable and creditable.

These 'rules' can be seen to be reflected in the professional body Code of Practice which we will now examine. The Code of Practice for Employees (GSCC, 2002) sets out the six precepts that all social care workers are expected to meet. This includes students because of their sponsorship by the Care Council, so it is important for you to become familiar with the following things that social care workers must do:

- Protect the rights and promote the interests of service users and carers.

- Strive to establish and maintain the trust and confidence of service users and carers.

- Promote the independence of service users while protecting them as far as possible from danger or harm.

- Respect the rights of service users while seeking to ensure that their behaviour does not harm themselves or other people.

- Uphold public trust and confidence in social care services.

- Be accountable for the quality of their work and take responsibility for maintaining and providing their knowledge and skills. (GSCC, 2002)

Each of these standards is broken into smaller explanations of what is expected of you as a social care worker. These reflect issues of good practice and often the kind of agency policy and procedures that you will come into contact with during your practice learning opportunities.

---

### ACTIVITY 1.2

*You will find the Code in full at the GSCC website, **www.gscc.org.uk/codes_ copies.htm**. You should download the Code of Practice and consider your values and beliefs identified in Activity 1.1 against the principles set out within the Code. Ask yourself what the Code of Practice might mean for you as a student social worker undertaking practice learning. Identify some of the difficulties that may arise.*

---

## Self-determination: ideal or possibility?

The question of self-determination often presents problems for student social workers in practice. Self-determination can be understood in two ways:

- as a positive freedom; or

- as a negative freedom.

Negative freedom suggests that people should be able to choose how to act and behave, whether to accept or refuse services without interference from others. This means that even if service users are at risk of self-harm they should be allowed to act in their chosen ways. The Code of Practice reflects the realities of social work practice, however, in curtailing self-determination, applying the concept of positive freedom which extends the choices people have over their lives wherever possible while recognising there are limitations and some people will need protection from harm by self or others. This approach necessitates acting in the 'best interests' of service users, which is a complex and difficult term. The concept may suggest a paternalistic approach and raise feelings of discomfort in you as a student social worker. It is important for you, therefore, to be aware of the following:

- the function and any statutory duty of your agency;

- how professional authority and power are used within the agency;

- the ethos of the agency (see Horne, 1999).

Also, asking questions about your discomfort might help. For example, a student in a child protection agency questioned the 'rights' of social workers to separate children from parents when neither the parents nor the child want this to happen. The practice teacher was able to present a case in which a child was at considerable physical risk if left in that situation and the student was able to weigh up whether the social workers should act against expressed interest or allow a child to be seriously harmed.

Values represent the core beliefs that gird social work practice. These are usually formulated in sets of principles and ethical codes such as the GSCC Code of Practice. For the social work student on practice learning the tasks of balancing rights and risks are assisted by the rules for practice. However, social workers in practice learning are also assessed on their development of anti-oppressive and anti-discriminatory practice to which we will now turn.

# Anti-discriminatory and anti-oppressive practice

## What is it?

There is considerable confusion among social work students, and, indeed, among qualified social workers, as to the meaning of anti-discriminatory and anti-oppressive practice. It is often asked whether the two are the same or have different and specific definitions. Neil Thompson (1997, p33) uses the term anti-discriminatory practice, describing it as follows:

*An approach to social work practice which seeks to reduce, undermine or eliminate discrimination or oppression specifically in terms of challenging sexism, racism, ageism and disablism, ... and other forms of discrimination or oppression encountered in social work. Social workers occupy positions of power and influence, and there is considerable scope for discrimination and oppression, whether this is intentional or by default. Anti-discriminatory practice is an attempt to eradicate discrimination and oppression from our own practice and challenge them in the practice of others and in the institutional structures in which we operate. In this respect it is a form of emancipatory practice.*

This understanding would seem to indicate that the two terms are interchangeable. However, Dalrymple and Burke (1995) warn against this assumption. They state that anti-discriminatory practice relates to specific challenges to certain forms of discrimination, often using legislation. An example here might relate to the ways in which the Disability Discrimination Act 1995 might be used to challenge a decision not to make reasonable adjustments to accommodate an employee who declares a disability.

Anti-oppressive practice, on the other hand, is taken to address wider structural issues and inequalities such as the way the worlds of work and schooling seem to favour the maintenance of different male and female roles.

The debate is not simply an academic one and may be seen as having far-reaching effects on our understanding of discrimination and oppression and, indeed, our practice as social workers. If you favour working solely in an anti-discriminatory way, tackling the impact of a particular form of discrimination resulting from age, gender, race and ethnicity, health status, ability or disability and so on, but ignore the impact of structural and social policy factors you may begin to rank in order of assumed importance or impact the different forms of discrimination. A hierarchy of oppression may be created in which polarised views become entrenched and certain forms of discrimination are considered worse or more severe than others. This is a useful tool for those who do not wish to see change and have something to gain or protect from preserving their advantaged position. It has the potential to set one group against another without addressing core issues. Of course, this does not mean that you should not seek to work in an anti-discriminatory way. It is important and central to learning in practice to challenge the focused abuse of power and exploitation of others using specific legislation, where available, and to consider the particular disadvantages resulting from a specific social division or difference.

## Some models of anti-oppressive practice

It is fundamental to set oppression and discrimination in a much wider perspective, understanding that oppression is experienced by individuals, groups and communities in diverse ways but from similar interacting elements including personal prejudices, but not exclusively so, that inform and are informed by the cultures of work and community in which people live, which interact with social factors to maintain the position of those in privileged locations in society. This is reflected in Thompson's PCS model of oppression (below).

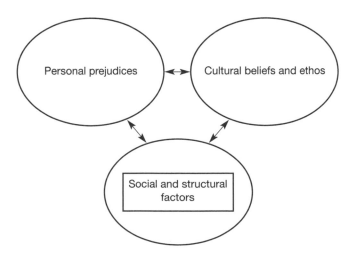

**Figure 1.2** *Thompson's PCS model of oppression (after Thompson, 1997)*

The concept suggests, for example, that personal prejudice alone does not explain racism. It is part of it and we may all have examples of racially prejudicial comments that we have found offensive. However, personal prejudice feeds into and from the setting in which it develops: the environment and neighbourhood in which it is found and within the schools, agencies and community groups within a particular location. In turn, the way that society is set up and runs informs how the environment operates and forms yet another influential factor in how discrimination and oppression on racial grounds develops. The personal, cultural and social aspects of life interact to create and recreate patterns of discrimination and oppression. It is important as a social work student undertaking practice learning to understand this within the context of the agency in which you are learning to practise.

---

ACTIVITY **1.3**

*Think back to your personal beliefs that you identified in Activity 1.1. Ask yourself how these might affect the work that you are undertaking in your agency. Also, consider the impact that your practice teacher/assessor has on your developing practice, the way you approach it and how you think about it. Use some of these reflections in supervision to consider together the development of values and the impact agencies have on these. List some possible outcomes for service users.*

---

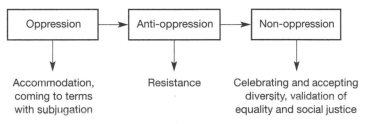

**Figure 1.3** *The continuum of oppression (after Dominelli, 2002)*

Dominelli (2002) understands oppression as a continuum that runs from oppression and exploitation through to empowerment and emancipation (see Figure 1.3). Before reaching such a positive outcome, those who are oppressed will resist and it is in this resistance that social workers can be effective in enabling people to challenge, campaign and change. In order to do this, social workers need to understand that oppression takes place within the social arena, and is (re)created by interactions between people in society. Social workers are important in working with people to reduce and eradicate oppression because they work with people in context. However, social workers are part of society and are involved in the interactions that create, recreate or resist oppression and, therefore, need continually to reflect on their position. As Dominelli (2002, p36), states:

*Anti-oppressive practice addresses the whole person and enables a practitioner to relate to his or her client's social context in a way that takes account of the 'allocative and authoritative resources' that both the practitioner and the client bring to the relationship. Thus, anti-oppressive practice takes on board personal, institutional, cultural and economic issues and examines how these impinge on individuals' behaviour and opportunities to develop their full potential as persons living within collective entities.*

A mystique has grown up around the terms, which has led some social workers not to question or challenge thinking and actions in a critical and reflective way for fear of appearing oppressive or discriminatory. This can lead to the very situation anti-oppressive and anti-discriminatory practices seek to reduce or eradicate. It is important for you to question why things are the way they are and the impact this has on yourself as a student practitioner, on your agency and on the people you are working with.

At the heart of social work lies a commitment to social justice and social change as well as improving the lot of individuals within society. The International Federation of Social Workers' definition of social work reflects this well (see p. vii).

## Some difficulties in being anti-oppressive in practice learning

### Social work is oppressive

Depending on the agency in which you are placed and its role and function, you may at some point question whether social work is itself oppressive. If you find yourself thinking so, you will need to reflect, first of all, on your understanding of values, ethics and anti-oppressive practice. This will help you to identify why you are thinking this way about social work. It will also help you to criticise your views and thinking and to challenge your agency where necessary.

---

**CASE STUDY**

*Peter was undertaking his first practice learning experience in a multi-disciplinary team for people with learning disabilities. One of the service users he was working with, James, had been self-harming and threatening his mother with a knife. This had reached a point of such seriousness that an assessment under the Mental Health Act 1983 was requested (see Johns, 2003; Golightley, 2004). The approved social worker for the team applied for James to be admitted to hospital under a section 2 for assessment after medical recommendations had been made. Peter felt uneasy about this decision, thinking that James should be able to make his own choices and really needed more one-to-one input, which was not available within the team. On reflection with his practice teacher, Peter recognised the possible harm to James and his mother if action had not been taken and the need to balance rights and risks in the context of service restraints.*

---

### My practice teacher is oppressive

When you are learning in practice, challenging someone who is acting as your 'teacher' and, at the end of your work there, your 'assessor' is difficult. A question often asked is, 'what do I do if I think my PT is oppressive?' This may relate to actions that your practice teacher/assessor has done, perhaps in not consulting with you or another person or taking advantage of you as 'another pair of hands in the office'. It may sometimes relate to things that your practice teacher/assessor has said, maybe telling a joke or making a remark that you find offensive. Remember, social workers are human beings too and you will find, despite the education social workers have received and despite the Codes of Practice to guide social work, that people can be oppressive.

The first thing to do is to tackle it at source if at all possible. Discuss your concerns openly with your practice teacher/assessor. State in a matter-of-fact way what you found oppressive and why. This will often allow you to debate issues and work through them. If this is not possible or does not work, take the 'lowest rung of the ladder' approach (see Figure 1.4). Your university will have given you advice on dealing with complaints or who to make contact with if something goes wrong while undertaking practice learning. This process should allow you to resolve the matter. Of course, if the incident cannot be resolved or is particularly serious it may be that the university's 'whistleblowing' procedure becomes necessary. This will be discussed later in this chapter.

Use the university complaints process and, where appropriate, 'whistle blowing' procedure

Talk to your university practice learning advisor or personal supervisor

Inform GSCC

Ask the university practice learning advisor to convene a meeting between yourself and your practice teacher

Talk to the person making the offensive remark. Explain your situation and seek resolution

**Figure 1.4** *The lowest rung on the ladder approach to problem-resolution*

### My clients are oppressive

> **CASE STUDY**
>
> *Ebenezer was told by the family he was visiting that they did not want his help or support because he would not understand their needs and they requested another worker. When he explored this further the family said they did not want a black man in their house.*
>
> *Ebenezer was shocked by so open a display of racism. He spoke with his practice teacher who advised him of the agency policy on equal opportunities and race equality, informing him that the agency would fully support him. They returned to the family together and explained the policies to them, advising that if they wanted a service it would be offered according to the equal opportunities policy. Also, Ebenezer and his practice teacher spent time reflecting on the impact of racism on him as a beginning professional and how he might deal with future situations.*

It is important when experiencing oppression and discrimination from service users that the agency position is made clear. However, when discrimination is directed personally at you as a student, as in Ebenezer's case, the agency has a duty of care to protect you from potential harm. You may need to be withdrawn from a situation which may result in a family or individual not receiving a service. Where discriminatory expressions are made that are not personally directed, they need to be tackled and situations which may cause offence should be pointed out and discussed. If not, then you may be condoning or giving implicit legitimacy to the views expressed. This is not easy and it is important that you discuss these issues with your practice teacher, working out ways together of communicating difficult messages to service users.

You can use Thompson's (1997) model of oppression and Dominelli's (2002) continuum to analyse your practice and to provide evidence of your developing anti-oppressive approach. Consider the people with whom you are working and reflect critically on your approach to them, the beliefs you hold about your service users and how this may impact upon them. Analyse the social and environmental situation in which service users find themselves, noting the barriers that may be in the way of changing that situation. Also, consider the role and function of the agency and the culture that has developed among staff within the agency. Are your service users aware of the impact of various social, environmental and community pressures? Are they resisting them and what are you doing to champion their rights and find ways in which their voices can be heard? By considering each of your cases in this way you will be able to build some reflective evidence demonstrating the development of anti-oppressive practice. This will be useful for self-assessment and also to share with your practice teacher/assessor (see Chapter 5).

# Whistleblowing/public interest disclosure

Whistleblowing has become enshrined as one of the principles of probity in public life. It has become accepted for two key reasons. Firstly, it is important to ensure that bad practice is not left unchallenged and to ensure that the public and care recipients do not suffer at the hands of uncaring, exploitative or incompetent practitioners. Secondly, it has been boosted by the actions of a brave few who have stood against bad practice and made it known when things have been going wrong.

All social work programmes are required to have 'whistleblowing' procedures as part of the validation of their degree by the GSCC. You should have access to yours on your student website, in your student or practice learning handbook or by some other accessible means. You will need to seek it out and be familiar with it since it makes some demands of you, and, indeed, offers you some protection when you are learning in an external practice agency. If you have not done so already, locate a copy of the procedure and note the key points that impact on you learning in practice. Also, identify the agency's public interest disclosure policy, highlight your responsibilities here and match them with the university procedure. Paying attention to such matters will help to structure early supervision sessions when you are getting to know the agency context

Making the decision to disclose bad or dangerous practice may have serious repercussions for you as a student on placement, for the agency and or workers about whom you disclose and for the university provider in finding and locating practice learning opportunities. However, it is fundamental that where you see poor practice that you bring it to the attention of those people named under the procedure – usually this will be either your practice teacher/assessor or your practice learning coordinator at the university.

Check who it is that you should first make contact with and they will be able to advise you on how to proceed. You should not be penalised for making a genuine disclosure, one which you believe to be true even if, after investigation, it proves not to be.

Sometimes it is the case that revealing bad practice in an agency leads to the practice learning opportunity being terminated. This may have the effect of extending your programme of study, of disrupting your pathway through the programme and seemingly penalising you for what is essentially good practice. You should check how the university and programme intends to support you when you make a disclosure.

# Termination of training

Social work programmes are necessarily demanding and challenging because it is important that people who use services and their carers – who, of course, may be any one of us – are protected from poor practice. Therefore, every programme has a procedure called by the GSCC a 'termination of training' procedure, though it may well be called by a different name in your university. This document will set out when a student's practice may lead to a disciplinary hearing, what penalties the student might incur and when a programme might remove a student from professional social work training. It will, of course, describe any appeal process and indicate when an appeal is not possible where this differs from the usual university processes.

These documents deal with matters of professional misconduct – doing something that is against the values of the profession for which the student is training – or professional unsuitability. The latter ground for ending a student's training depends on the professional judgement of those deciding the matter. As you will remember, when you started your programme you will have signed a declaration concerning your fitness on health grounds to train as a social worker. This is open to change during your programme and your responsibilities are to ensure that you do not practise if you are suffering from a condition that might put you or your service users in a vulnerable or risk situation. These matters are often temporary and do not necessarily preclude you from continuing your studies. However, it is important that you tell your supervisor at university and your practice teacher when on practice learning if something arises that may be significant. To do so demonstrates professional practice, while not to do so may reflect unprofessional practice and raise the question of suitability.

It is not just health matters that are covered under matters of professional suitability and fitness to practise. Conduct and behaviour generally, while studying at university and in particular while undertaking practice learning, must fall within the parameters of acceptable professional standards. Your behaviour must not, for instance, deliberately flout the policies and procedures of the agency, unless these represent poor practice and you are highlighting them using the 'whistleblowing' process described above.

The procedure for ending your involvement in the programme will probably have a number of stages to it depending on the nature and degree of the allegation of misconduct or professional unsuitability. It may perhaps indicate that a precautionary suspension from placement is indicated while investigations take place and it may offer a number of levels of resolution with the most extreme being termination from the programme.

Decisions under this process are not taken lightly. Following the Code of Practice for Employers (GSCC, 2002) and acting in a way that upholds the values of social work will protect you from falling foul of the procedure.

# Negotiating your way: checking your development and providing evidence of values in practice

We have explored, so far, some of the complexities of values, ethical codes and anti-oppressive practice in social work, and looked at the procedural requirements in the degree that help to guide practice. The way you develop and demonstrate values in practice is a core element of your assessment as a fit practitioner and it will be, in the main, up to you to provide evidence to indicate that you have learned and applied professional values and ethics in your practice. In this section we will explore some of the ways in which you might gather and present such evidence. Here, we are taking the view that your developing competence in value-based and ethical practice is assessed in three ways: at a summative, formative and reflective level, as shown in Figure 1.5 (see further discussion of this assessment model in Chapter 5).

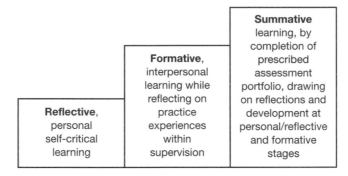

*Figure 1.5* *Levels of assessment in value-based practice*

## Summative assessment

It is likely that your social work programme will ask that you develop a portfolio of evidence to demonstrate how successful you have been in meeting the competences and standards required for practice learning (see Chapter 5). Part of this portfolio will refer to values and ethics in social work and will ask you to provide evidence concerning the development and demonstration of social work values in practice. It is important, therefore, that you collect evidence throughout the practice learning opportunity to include later. It is also important to share these reflections with your practice teacher/assessor in order to check your development regularly.

## Formative assessment

The first formal point of assessment will be the supervision sessions in which you engage with your practice teacher or assessor. Supervision will be explored in detail in Chapter 4 but the regular, formal and informal contact that you have with a nominated and experienced person within the agency will be central to confirming your development and progress and highlighting areas of learning need or areas in which you are struggling.

## Reflective assessment

One way of preparing for supervision in which values and practice will form part of the discussion is to record evidence from your practice. As with any recording, it is always best to do so as soon after the event you are writing about as possible. This will prevent you overlaying your thoughts about the event, piece of practice or situation with other experiences that might give you a different understanding. This kind of reflection is important later on but contemporaneous recording will help you to chart your development.

Whichever social work programme you are studying, the GSCC Code of Practice will form a central element when assessing the development of ethical practice. The Code is not, as we have seen, the exclusive fount of values and ethics in social work, and it is likely that you will be expected to demonstrate knowledge of and competence in working with other core social work values. The example of a way of recording your development shown in Figure 1.6, formed by combining the GSCC precepts and the eight principles or 'rules' for practice outlined by Clark (2000), provides a first step in reflecting on your progress.

| | • Protect the rights and promote the interests of service user's and carers • Strive to establish and maintain the trust and confidence of service users and carers • Promote the independence of service users while protecting them as far as possible from danger or harm • Respect the rights of service users while seeking to ensure that their behaviour does not harm themselves or other people • Uphold public trust and confidence in social care services • Be accountable for the quality of their work and take responsibility for maintaining and providing their knowledge and skills | • Respectfulness • Honesty and truthfulness • Being knowledgeable and skilful • Being careful and diligent • Being effective and helpful • Being legitimate and authorised • Being collaborative and accountable • Being reputable and creditable |
|---|---|---|
| What was the event or situation? | | |
| What did you learn? | | |

*Figure 1.6* *Checking values in practice*

Asking yourself the questions in the left-hand column will focus your thoughts on the situation you were involved in. Having done so you will be able to appraise what you did in the light of the Code of Practice (see the middle column). For instance, was the situation one of protection of rights and advocacy or protection from harm? Were you clear, honest and upfront about your reasons for being involved and how did you ensure that service users knew what your role and tasks were? You can then consider your practice against the core principles outlined by Clark (2000) in the final column.

If you do this for each of the questions in the left-hand column you will begin to build up a useful body of evidence demonstrating the development of your values during practice learning.

## C H A P T E R   S U M M A R Y

In this chapter you have considered the complexities of values, anti-oppressive approaches and ethical codes in guiding social work practice. Some of the ways in which values and ethics will impact on your practice learning and how you might begin to monitor and evaluate your development have also been explored.

Core principles represent a cornerstone of good social work practice. There are no easy answers to many of the ethical dilemmas with which social work students and, indeed, qualified practitioners come into contact. But developing a systematic approach to analysing your values and reflecting critically on your practice will help you, at this stage, to meet the requirements for practice contained within the social work degree and, in future practice, to continue your professional development.

**FURTHER READING**

**Clark, C.** (2000) Social Work Ethics: Politics, Principles and Practice. Basingstoke: Palgrave Macmillan.
While Clark's book deals with some complex concepts and philosophical issues, it will provide you with an all round introduction to values and ethical principles in social work practice.

**Dominelli, L.** (2002) Anti-Oppressive Social Work Theory and Practice. Basingstoke: Palgrave Macmillan.
This is by far the most comprehensive and well-argued text on anti-oppressive social work practice. Concepts are clearly explained and in-depth theoretical underpinnings are given.

**GSCC** (2002) Code of Practice for Employers. London: GSCC.
You should keep in mind the Code of Practice as you progress through your practice, checking its precepts against values for practice.

# Chapter 2

## Integrating theory and developing reflective practice in practice learning

## Introduction

A monumental challenge for many students concerns the use of theories, methods, frameworks and models in practice settings. So often students – and indeed practitioners – will avoid theories, state that they do not see their relevance or, even, actively renounce them. However, theories and models guide social workers' actions and provide explanatory frameworks that make effective interventions possible and, in doing so, they contribute to ethical, evidence-based and accountable practice. In the first part of this chapter, we will consider what we mean by the terms theories, models and frameworks for practice before examining some of the barriers to using them in practice. We will seek ways of overcoming these obstacles. The practical relevance of theory will be emphasised and the ethical reasons for its use and development will be promoted.

Indeed, the requirements set out for the degree in social work continually emphasise the need for social workers to be able to apply theories, models and frameworks in their practice. It is the responsibility of your programme to:

*ensure that the teaching of theoretical knowledge, skills and values is based on their application in practice.*

(Department of Health, 2002, p3)

Developing a reflective approach to learning has become an important area of much professional learning (Tate and Sills, 2004), and no less so in social work despite it being a somewhat contentious concept (Ixer, 1999, 2003). The latter part of this chapter will consider the development of reflective practice and learning, describe models of reflection in practice, for practice and about practice, and seek, using a range of reflective activities, to assist students in becoming reflective in their learning.

Barriers to the development of reflective practice will be discussed and alternative ways of encouraging reflection will be explored. Links will be made within this chapter to other chapters in the book.

The concept of reflective practice is not an easy one to grasp but it is considered central to many aspects of learning for practice. Therefore, this chapter necessarily includes some complex material, concepts and theories. However, you should stay with this and check your understanding throughout.

# What are theories, models and frameworks for practice?

There has been a tendency to see theory and practice as representing different things, and that you can, indeed, have one without the other. Fook (2002, p38) sees the split between theory and practice as dangerous.

*The separate worlds of theory and practice have been built in this way in line with the hierarchical split between professionals and service users and researchers and practitioners. Constructing theory and practice as separate entities, and privileging one over the other, seems to preserve a dominance of researcher over practitioner views and professional over service user perspectives.*

She sees a complex, intermingled relationship between theory and practice as important in promoting partnerships and participation in social work and in redressing some of the existing power imbalance in social work relationships. The relevance of theory to the practice of social work lies in its potential to inform and improve practice by suggesting what could be done in certain social work situations or at least providing a framework for understanding the situations of service users. However, students have often denigrated the use of theory (Parker, 1999), suggesting that theory objectifies and impersonalises practice. Coulshed and Orme (1998, p7) summarise this well:

*In social work there has always been a tension between practice and theory. At times students and practitioners have protested that it was necessary to forget theory once in practice placements, that it reduced spontaneity in caring for people.*

Such a view is unethical as it would suggest that research into effective practice and the harnessed wisdom of an experienced social worker are not relevant. There would be no structure or direction to social work if that were the case and such views needs to change. It is worth examining what we might mean by 'theory'.

A useful way of conceptualising theory is offered by Payne (1997) who adapts Sibeon's (1990) distinction between formal and informal theory, suggesting that there are three types of theory:

- theories of what social work is;

- theories of how to do social work;

- theories of the service user's world.

These three types of theory can be considered in formal terms or informally with regard to how social workers develop and use theories derived from experience. You are likely to use all three types in your practice learning and to do so in both ways. For instance, you will have a particular view about social welfare, whether that is informed by a particular socio-logical, religious or political position or has developed from your experiences of the world and social work.

Also, you are going to practise in a certain way depending on the agency in which you undertake your practice learning. Where this does not follow a clearly defined or explicit model, you should seek to identify and explore what is done, how and why. You are likely also to use theories about family, childcare, ageing, gender and so on in understanding the experiences of service users. This typology of theories helps us in understanding some of the varied terms that are used. In this chapter, theories, methods, models and frameworks for practice are used interchangeably. However, it is possible to define them by level. Theory relates to explanations of what social work is or how people age and develop, while meth-ods, models and frameworks may relate more to what social workers do.

In practice learning, you will no doubt be concentrating on 'theories of how to do social work', which is something that your practice teachers and university will want to assess. It is also something that should be appreciated by service users if your learning assists in developing knowledge and skills in applying models of intervention that meet people's needs. You will also focus on 'theories of the service user's world' by demonstrating understanding of the impact of social, economic and political factors on a person's life, or by being able to apply knowledge of stages of development.

What is important is to ensure that you acknowledge your approaches, thinking and theo-rising and begin to become more aware of the use and impact of formal theory in practice. This is likely to draw on learning for practice that you have undertaken prior to starting your practice learning. We will now turn to consider how theories and knowledge are used in social work practice.

# Evidence concerning the use of theories, models and frameworks in social work practice

The Social Care Institute for Excellence (SCIE) review of knowledge in social care recognised that practitioner knowledge is usually passed on in a tacit way and acquired through practice and sharing collective wisdom, through training and formal and informal consultation, rather than judged against any specific standards (Pawson et al., 2003). Practice wisdom and working intuitively lie at the heart of reflective practice, which underpins much of what social workers do and how their practice develops, and we shall consider this later in the chapter. However, as Munro (1998, p89) points out, this 'preference for a personal, private style of working is a major obstacle to changing their use of theories and evaluating practice.'

Whatever we do is, to some extent, based on theory. It relates to our interpretations of past experiences, our value base and beliefs and, for social work students, the education programme being studied (Preston-Shoot and Agass, 1990). However, it is important, as Thompson (2000) points out, that we manage the process of integrating theory with practice because this will help guard against perpetuating mistakes. Integrating theory in practice will help in developing one's professional practice. Thompson (2000, p94) states that we need to take control of the fusion of practice and theory so we can:

- be conscious of the potential for bias and discrimination;

- make the best and most constructive use of the knowledge available;

- maximise opportunities for learning (and, indirectly, job satisfaction);

- challenge and develop the knowledge base;

- avoid the mistakes of the past.

---

**ACTIVITY 2.1**

*Why do you think that some social workers and students find it difficult to use theories in practice?*

*In answering this question you may have suggested that the way theory is defined and understood may put people off, or that the complexity and difficulty in making theories accessible discourage its use. It may be that you have identified that some people consider practice to be unconnected with theory.*

---

There are many reasons why people may not use theory but let us return briefly to Thompson's rationale for merging practice and theory and ways in which theory and practice can be better integrated.

# Effective integration of theories and models in practice

Pawson et al. (2003, p40) suggest that asking the question TAPUPA is helpful for social workers in analysing knowledge for practice. The acronym stands for:

**T**ransparency – is it open to scrutiny?

**A**ccuracy – is it well grounded?

**P**urposivity – is it fit for purpose?

**U**tility – is it fit for use?

**P**ropriety – is it legal and ethical?

**A**ccessibility – is it intelligible?

When you reflect on theories, knowledge and research in your practice it will be useful to apply these questions to it. While this is not a fail-safe mechanism for applying and under-standing knowledge for practice, it provides a way of scrutinising what relevance the knowledge has and gives you a chance to reflect on the impact of using that knowledge.

Thompson (2000) provides a valuable approach to integrating theory in practice. He is clear that to do this does not relate to a simple, mechanistic process. It is not something that can be easily taught and, as a student social worker, you will need to engage with the process in an active way when considering your thoughts about your work, the actions you are engaged in and the values which you bring to your practice as a social work stu-dent (see Chapter 1).

Thompson identifies 15 strategies for integrating theory and practice that rely on the fos-tering of reflective practice to which we will turn later in this chapter. These strategies are:

- using cycles of learning;
- going beyond practice wisdom;
- going beyond theory-less practice;
- going beyond common sense;
- developing research-minded practice;
- going beyond elitism and anti-intellectualism;
- using the critical incident technique;
- developing a group approach;
- promoting continuous professional development;
- developing interprofessional learning;
- using mentoring;
- problematising;

- using enquiry and action learning;

- balancing challenge and support;

- developing staff care.

We will consider some of these strategies for assisting your integration of theory and practice in practice learning.

The *cycle of learning* relates to a process of experience, reflection, conceptualisation and active experimentation and will be considered in more depth later in this chapter. In your practice, this kind of reflective learning will be central to your development. However, it is possible to use this process to scrutinise, challenge and refine the ways in which you use knowledge and theory in practice. For instance, if you were working with someone using a task-centred approach (see Parker and Bradley, 2003) you would need to consider what you did in using the model, what the effects or outcomes were, what alternative explanations there might be and how you might use this experience in future practice. Then you would be able to experiment using your experiential knowledge.

As a student, you need to *go beyond practice wisdom* and *common sense*, or intuitively and uncritically act, without making conscious and systematic efforts to critique and hone your understanding and subsequent practice. This is where use of the cycle of learning can be important. It also guards against the mistaken assumption that practice can be *theory-less*. Everything you do is based on some assumptions that you have made about what might be happening or needed, even if these do not fit with a particular model or theory.

As a social work student you will have been introduced to the concept of the *research-minded* practitioner in which you act, critically analyse and reflect on the rationale for the actions you have taken to produce an evidence-based understanding. Social work practice is, in many respects, not dissimilar to research. Both seek to develop understanding and test out predictions. Developing research-minded practice looks at the processes of practice.

One important way of maximising the potential for integrating theory and practice during practice learning is to use the supervision session (see Chapter 4). It is possible and valuable to develop reflective practice and theory logs in individual supervision sessions (see later in the chapter).

As well as individual sessions, it is helpful in practice learning supervision sessions to adopt a discursive group approach to theory–practice integration. This can be facilitated in a number of ways that might draw upon Thompson's strategies. A *learning set* or group focused around learning about practice allows you as adult learners to take responsibility for the process of reflection, critique, development and further practice. Such an approach might stem from discussing a *critical incident*: identifying what happened in a given situation and how this might be explained or understood, and what theoretical frameworks might be helpful in understanding the incident and guiding future practice.

If you are working in a *multi-disciplinary or multi-professional team*, it can be illuminating to open up the learning set to a range of students undertaking different professional education. This allows for the debate of theory and practice to be set in different contexts and provides you, as a social work student, with opportunities to gain knowledge and understanding of the ways in which other professionals use theory in practice.

Many universities operate a 'call-back' system for students undertaking practice learning. This is extremely valuable in assisting your university to fulfil its obligation to ensure that your theoretical learning is applied appropriately to practice, and also important to you in sharing your learning with other social work students. Call-back days operate in diverse ways within different universities. They offer the opportunity to consider incidents, to develop learning sets and to apply a cycle of learning approach to your development. If your university does not operate such a system it is possible, of course, for you as an adult learner to take responsibility for coordinating, developing and running such a learning group. With the advance of information and communication technologies it is often possible to set up an electronic discussion group to share your learning and ways in which you might integrate theory with practice.

Perhaps the commonest approach to developing theory–practice integration stems from an *enquiry and action* learning method (Burgess and Jackson, 1990; Taylor and Burgess, 1995). This is similar to problem-based learning in medicine and healthcare education but is a method developed with social work in mind. Study using this method builds around a case study or problem area which students work on to resolve. The method involves formal teaching and learning, and in practice learning this may come from either the university or your practice teacher or other designated practitioner. However, the process of search and discovery is integral to the learning gained in this model. You, as a social work student, will take responsibility for finding out information about the situation or case and the knowledge and research relevant to it. You will also identify, test, apply and reflect on ways of intervening to change the situation.

Noble (2001) reports on a research project with final-year social work students in Australia that highlights the potential use of student-centred narratives as a way of integrating theory and practice. Students used a 'theory-in-action' model of learning, completing a reflective practice workbook that used their practice experiences as a focus for reflection and reordering of their thoughts and actions. The research explored some of the ways in which students identified and used connections between the world of theory and the world of practice. The workbook used narratives as a way of developing a critical reflective focus.

Narratives are understood as a form of student-centred learning that allow the power of the student voice in his or her learning to be heard and links to be made with the personal and developing professional self.

Students completed a three-framework workbook that considered critical incidents, 'theory-in-action' reflections and narration of an experience or event. In the last framework students were asked to write a story in the first person where the search for meaning was central to the narrative. The narratives were brought to and explored within the classroom to allow deeper reflection and comparison.

Social work practice is driven by theory, some taken from formal knowledge that you will have learned and should continue to read about. This might include knowledge about people and practice such as attachment theory, loss and bereavement, families and parenting. It may also include knowledge about how to practice, such as using task-centred approaches, cognitive-behavioural methods or person-centred and humanistic models. In your practice learning you will be expected to show and use this knowledge, depending on the particular practice agency's function and remit. However, you will also begin to construct a body of informal knowledge, or experiential wisdom, from working with people in practice. Making your use of theory and knowledge explicit and acknowledging the need for continuous development is important. In the remaining part of this chapter, we will introduce the concept of reflective practice which will be instrumental in helping you to integrate theory into your practice learning.

# The development of reflective practice

It is important to understand how the concept of reflection took hold in professional education to inform how we approach and use it in developing learning as a social worker. The concept became firmly embedded in social work education throughout the latter half of the twentieth century and has also become central to adult learning within professional training. Tate and Sills (2004) have collected together a compendium of reflective practice in many of the health professions, including podiatry, physiotherapy, pharmacy, occupational therapy, midwifery and nursing to name a few, that demonstrates the wide acceptance of the concept. This section will introduce you to some of the historical and developmental background before we seek to define reflective practice and its processes more clearly.

The beginnings of reflective practice in education is generally traced back to the work of the educational philosopher, John Dewey. Dewey (1933, 1938) suggested that people only begin to reflect when they identify an issue as a problem to be overcome and recognise that this can create an air of uncertainty about the outcome. Dewey considered reflection to represent the continual re-evaluation or taking stock of personal beliefs, assumptions and hypotheses in the light of experience and data and the generation of alternative interpretations of those experiences and data. This is a practical problem-solving approach that Ixer (1999) categorises as pragmatism. Dewey's ideas can be represented by a five-stage model that Ixer suggests can be modified for use in social work:

1. It is only possible to reflect authentically when a person identifies a problem that is perplexing and 'felt'. (This can provide a pointer for organising assessment in practice, of acknowledging what experiences are leading to issues and problems that need to be worked on.)

2. The identified problem is observed and refined to create fuller understanding.

3. The person reflecting begins to develop a hypothesis about the problem, how it came about, what alternative understandings there might be and what possible solutions might be found. (Social work students may act too quickly here. If you are using this process to structure your reflections you need to remain aware that this stage represents a beginning process and solutions are tentative and require testing.)

4. The hypothesis is then subjected to scrutiny and reasoning. This part of the process prefigures the transformation of knowledge that is implicit into a process that is deliberate and conscious.

**5.** The final stage concerns corroboration by testing the hypothesis or understanding in practice. (This is used often by social worker students undertaking practice learning. You will be asked to monitor your practice and what happens when you undertake certain actions under certain circumstances.)

The following case study provides an example of how this model might work in practice.

---

**CASE STUDY**

*Graham was uneasy about making assessments of need using the eligibility criteria for services set by his agency. He discussed this discomfort with his practice teacher and suggested that he felt this way because eligibility criteria set limits against people's needs and he believed strongly that needs were perceived individually. For Graham, his objection was based on values and principles. The practice teacher reflected some sympathy with this perspective but assisted Graham in considering why eligibility criteria were set and what outcomes there were for those receiving an assessment or service and for those who did not. They then began examining what options there were for meeting people's needs in different ways. Graham was able to understand that some 'gatekeeping' measures were important in planning and delivering welfare not only to keep costs down but also to ensure that people needing a service as a priority were able to receive one. In discussion with his practice teacher he also identified the information and advice-giving role of social work as important in helping people who did not meet the criteria to find alternative support. Graham's key learning was to find out about local resources, contacts and means of access in some depth.*

---

In philosophical terms, Ixer (1999) indicates that there are two conceptual levels operating in Dewey's problem-solving approach to reflective practice. One is taken from the work of seventeenth-century philosopher Immanuel Kant and his notion of 'pure reason'. This relates to developing analytical thought and rational deduction. The other relates to the interpretation of one's experiences. He suggests that moving between the two offers a way of understanding the process. In Graham's case above, the discussion with his practice teacher helped him to analyse and comment on the situation while his interpretation of what might be done was based around his values and experiences in practice.

It is Schön (1983, 1987) who is usually credited with the wider development and increasing the popularity of reflective practice in adult learning. His work took forward the thinking of Dewey. Schön (1983) describes the process of change and understanding in professional learning and development from a 'technical-rational' approach to an approach based on 'reflection-in-action'. The technical-rational approach suggests that learning for professional practice concerns the deployment of problem-solving skills based on scientific principles in which the problem always responds in the same way to the same actions. It concerns a belief that if there is agreement about ends and outcomes, then what one ought to do to get there can be reduced to an instrumental question about the best means to achieve that agreed end. A simplified example of this approach might be drawn from medical learning and practice in which a junior surgeon is shown how to make a particular incision to begin an appendectomy. The junior surgeon later undertakes this procedure and subsequently demonstrates the procedure to another junior doctor. The activity and knowledge for this student was passed on from teacher to student as a given way of performing this task. In social work, a technical-rational approach would suggest that using intervention A (for example, a method of behaviour management), which can be taught in the classroom, can be applied in the same way in a specified situation (such as monitoring and reducing drinking) to produce an expected outcome (only drinking in moderation to the recommended safe limits). However, Schön believes that human professional activity such as social work demands a different approach.

The limits to technical rationality began to be observed after the Second World War. Professions have not always lived up to their norms and standards and the environment in which problems have arisen has become recognised as important in how we choose a problem to address. How we think about or recognise an issue or problem is important in determining how we address it.

When there are conflicting views about practice, as in social work, different ways of establishing problem-setting as well as solutions emerge. Schön's view is that the technical-rational model fails to account for practice competence in diverse situations and proposes a model that celebrates the intuitive and artistic approaches that can be brought to uncertain and shifting situations. He calls this 'reflection-in-action', which he links to the everyday knowledge we bring to everyday situations in life:

> When we go about the spontaneous, intuitive performance of the actions of everyday life, we show ourselves to be knowledgeable in a special way. Often we cannot say what it is that we know. When we try to describe it we find ourselves at a loss, or we produce descriptions that are obviously inappropriate. Our knowing is ordinarily tacit, implicit in our patterns of action and in our feel for the stuff with which we are dealing. It seems right to say that our knowing is in our action.
>
> (Schön, 2002, p50)

'Knowing in action' describes the knowledge that one shows in practice which cannot be described beforehand. Reflection in action concerns thinking about something while engaged in doing it, having a 'feel' for something and practising according to this 'feel'.

Professional practice concerns what the social worker does. It concerns performance, preparation for performance and repetition of performance through which expectations and predictions emerge. Reflection is important in critiquing the understandings that develop around repeated practice to make new sense of situations and to prevent stagnant responses:

> When someone reflects-in-action, he becomes a researcher in the practice context. He is not dependent on the categories of established theory and technique, but constructs a new theory of the unique case.
>
> (Schön, 2002, p59)

The model is not without criticism and it is important to stress that formal learning remains important. Tate (2004) believes that both forms of knowledge, technical rationality and professional artistry, are involved in learning to become a professional but stresses that artistry links the two. Ixer (1999) believes that the time factor was not considered as significant by Schön who thought that a person could continue 'doing' while reflecting and altering or refining practice. Eraut (1995) suggested that when a person begins the process of inward reflection this involves leaving, albeit in a thinking or cognitive sense, the action or setting in which the issue reflected on was taking place. It is not a process that happens instantaneously alongside whatever is the subject of the reflection, even if the person doing the reflecting is still physically in that setting. Any action that takes place in that context may involve 'tacit knowledge', meaning that the knowledge and rationale underpinning what was done cannot be theorised or described explicitly. In order to move from this essentially passive state would require the person to take control of his or her thinking and the reasons for acting in a certain way – 'process knowledge'. This kind of thinking and reflection is set apart from the time frame of what is happening and is guided by the individual's preconceived ideas and interpretations of them.

# Caveats and understanding

Ixer (1999) provides a useful corrective to the often uncritical attention paid to developing and assessing reflective practice in social work learning. He points out that definitions of reflective practice are problematic and theoretical explanations developed so far are open to debate. The main concern Ixer raises is that you as a social work student may be vulnerable to poor learning experiences if practice teachers and universities have poorly constructed and varying conceptions of reflective practice. Confusion will arise unless there is agreement on the use of the term and how it is to be demonstrated and used in the practice setting. He suggests that reflection may not be open to adequate assessment until we can all state clearly what reflection means.

---

*ACTIVITY* **2.2**

*Think about your understanding of reflective practice. Write down what it means to you, how you might go about the process and what the purpose of reflection might be. Share these thoughts with your practice teacher and ask him or her to explain what they mean by reflective practice, how it operates and what is its purpose. Identify any similarities and differences and use these to construct a common understanding of reflective practice that you can use and develop throughout the practice learning experience.*

---

Social work practice for Ixer (1999) requires more than a passive reflection on action, but immediate cognitive processing that enables a judgement to be made that is followed by making decisions and acting. This takes the social worker beyond Schön's description of reflective practice and it is important to remember this in practice learning, as this end outcome is the one that you will be hoping to achieve and, indeed, are likely to be assessed upon. Therefore some agreement needs to be reached to view reflection in this way. While Ixer suggests that practice teachers need to be wary of assessing reflection in students as an outcome, so too do you as a student social worker. Reflection is not something that is open to reductionist assessment techniques such as ticking a box once completed. It represents the continual creation of new ideas, ways of thinking and actions. As Tate (2004) suggests, we learn through critical reflection by putting ourselves into the experience and exploring theoretical and personal knowledge to understand it and view it in different ways. Reflection seeks to transform the way we approach matters and to use knowledge exploration to learn and develop. Ixer (1999, p523) states:

*Reflection aims to develop conscious control of knowledge ..., through a process of metacognition, so that professionals are able to self-analyse and learn to operate more effectively in demanding situations. In essence, this means that they develop transferable skills which are life-long and not context-specific. This is the real substance behind reflection.*

You will, however, be assessed on your ability to reflect on your learning and practice and you will, no doubt, be encouraged to engage in self-reflection. Fade (2004), writing for dieticians, recognises some of the difficulties brought to the fore by Ixer, but suggests that assessment of reflection depends to a large extent on your practice teacher and university providing you with broad-based assessment criteria that allow you to reflect as an individual but offer guidance as to what is expected. It is important, therefore, that you agree with your practice teacher or assessor what reflective practice means to you both and how you will use it in promoting your development.

Nathan (2002) offers a positive view of reflection when employed appropriately for learning, but his work is based on qualified practitioners. Nathan suggests that the concept of reflection sits neatly between the demands of the agency and academy (see Figure 2.1). He would argue that social workers know more than they can state in clear terms, something akin to 'tacit knowledge' as identified by Schön, and considered it to represent an example of practice competence when such knowledge and skills are demonstrated in action. The point at which one becomes a reflective practitioner is when that tacit knowledge is made explicit. So, for Nathan (2002, pp67–8), a reflective practitioner is:

*A practitioner who has the capacity to translate the knowing and reflection-in-action from a tacit knowledge, based on learned intuition, into a form of practice knowledge that includes reflection on that practice, where that knowledge is explicit and articulated. What is termed explicit knowledge.*

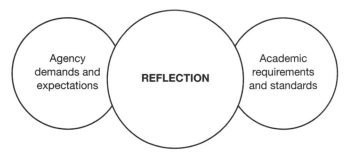

*Figure 2.1* *Reflection in practice (after Nathan, 2002)*

One strategy that Nathan uses to create this transition in knowledge is to encourage post-qualifying students to share their work and reflections with others on the course. This is a high-level skill, however, and one that needs approaching with care during qualifying education. It may be, however, that your university expects this kind of sharing and reflection in call-back days during your practice learning opportunity. You should, therefore, be prepared to open your practice to the scrutiny of others and acknowledge constructive feedback in a positive way.

# Models of reflective practice

There is a variety of models for reflective practice. It is important to remember, however, that reflection is a process and, as such, it cannot be bound and described by a single model. However, models are useful devices when it comes to building strategies for learning in practice learning. Ixer (2003) recognises that social work values are integral to the ways in which social workers reflect. Values should, therefore, be central to your reflections on practice (see Chapter 1). He uses Issitt's (1999) model of anti-oppressive reflective practice, a kind of reflection on values-in-action, to suggest a way forward in the teaching of values in practice learning. He proposes 13 guidelines for developing effective reflective practice:

1. Discuss and agree on a model or understanding of reflection from which both student and practice teacher can work.

2. Reflection should involve four interrelated characteristics – cognition, affect, morality, creativity.

3. Reflection is a process skill that allows you to look internally at the way you learn and to reflect on your own reflection.

4. Race, gender, sexual orientation and other social constructs should be continually acknowledged.

5. Reflection can be painful and requires non-judgemental support.

6. Reflection is mutual and practice teachers should be able to reflect and lead by example.

7. The essence of integrating values with reflection is to encourage open and critical dialogue.

8. Your success in reflection will depend to a large extent on the degree of openness between yourself and the practice teacher.

9. You need to feel safe enough to reflect or you might engage in 'expedient learning' – doing what you expect will get you through.

10. Reflection should be seen as a process in its own right.

11. You should use as many ways as possible of developing reflection, and using narratives can be helpful.

12. The process should allow you to explore and identify your own values through the reflective process.

13. Reflection can best be measured by evaluating the degree to which you can articulate your own reflection on reflection and describe the process as well as in terms of outcomes.

Tate (2004) believes also that reflective approaches to learning are flexible enough to be undertaken individually, in pairs or in groups and so it represents a useful process for social work practice learning.

Many of the models that have been developed and adapted for use in social work derive from Kolb's learning cycle (Kolb, 1984) and from the work of Boud et al. (1985) (see also Gould and Taylor, 1996).

## Kolb's learning cycle

This model of learning has become central to practice learning. It is based on the premise that experiences gained through life and work are crucial to learning, and this kind of experiential approach now forms part of most practice learning experiences and work-based learning programmes. Fry et al. (2003, p14) state that:

> *Experiential learning is based on the notion that understanding is not a fixed or unchangeable element of thought but is formed and re-formed through 'experience'. It is also a continuous process, often represented as cyclical, and, being based on experience, implies that we all bring to learning situations our own ideas and beliefs at different levels of elaboration.*

The model Kolb has developed is, therefore, cyclical. It relies on four abilities to learn from experience that stem from thinking on reflective practice (Kolb, 1984). These are shown in Figure 2.2.

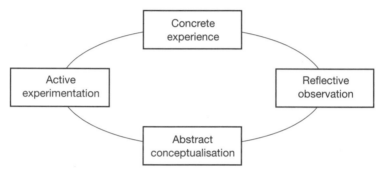

*Figure 2.2 Kolb's cycle of learning*

The model demands time and constructive feedback to work. While you will be able to consider your experiences and incidents occurring during your practice learning experience it is imperative that you seek the support and guidance of your practice teacher to consider these experiences from a range of perspectives. For instance, let us imagine that you have returned from a visit to family who actively sought support in caring for a grandmother who had recently been diagnosed with dementia and was leaving the house on her own two or three times each night. During your visit you are surprised by the anger and apparent hostility you receive from the woman's daughter, although the initial referral came from her. She complains that you are not helping and that you do not understand her situation. It is this reaction that you take back from the visit as a 'concrete experience'. In order to process the situation you need time and should actively set aside part of your working day to reflect and theorise. Reflective observation requires you to consider what has happened from a wide variety of perspectives. On one level, you may assess the situation by concentrating solely on the reaction and its affect on you. You may also reflect on the shock and concern felt by the daughter who perhaps for the first time has been able to express this in words and directs her hurt and confusion at you as anger. While you will be able to identify a number of alternatives, you will maximise your reflections and understanding by sharing these and debating them with your practice teacher.

The third part of the process, abstract conceptualisation, relates to you being able to repackage and process the ideas that you have formed about the experience into a logical theoretical understanding. You may theorise in this instance that the daughter is dealing with the enormity of her situation by actively seeking help but processing the change in her situation and life by externalising the problem until it becomes manageable enough for her to integrate. This involves you acting as a sounding board, listening to her concerns and anger and helping her to process this in her own time. This might give you some understanding of the situation, and it will help you in integrating theory into practice as part of your learning as discussed earlier in this chapter.

However, practice learning is, by its very nature, practical, and this kind of reflection is helpful in providing you with plans and ideas to take forward your learning in practice settings. Armed with your understanding of the situation you may have planned with your practice teacher to provide a forum in which the daughter can explore her fears, wants and wishes in respect of her mother. You may also provide information and contacts for advice while she works through some of the thoughts and emotions about her mother's diagnosis and needs.

Your learning does not stop at this point, according to Kolb's model. It is, as we have noted, cyclical and by implementing the plans you have agreed with your practice teacher you would restart the process of experiencing, reflecting, conceptualising and experimenting.

## Experiential learning

The model constructed by Boud et al. (1985) is also particularly valuable for social work education as it integrates many different aspects of the learning process. It is similar to Kolb's model but attends to a more holistic approach to learning from experience, considering the emotional impact of events as well as the cognitive processes involved in learning. It involves returning to an event, incident or experience, considering the process in detail at an emotional and cognitive level and then re-evaluating the experience in the light of experience, knowledge from other sources and experimentation. The aim of the model is to make the re-evaluated learning one's own. The model is contained in Figure 2.3 (overleaf).

The processes involved are much akin to those in Kolb's model but, if you consider your work with the woman mentioned above, you would be encouraged to explore the emotional impact and to develop ways of integrating strategies to deal with this in your practice.

## Tips for developing reflective practice to assist your learning

The theory underpinning reflective practice and the models that have been developed are important to your learning but are complex. The key issue that we have stressed throughout the chapter is that you agree with your practice teacher how reflective practice will be understood and assessed, in line, of course, with your programme requirements. There are, however, some tools that you can use to maximise the potential learning you can gain from reflection that will also indicate development and identify future learning needs as you progress through your practice learning experiences.

| The event, situation or experience | **Returning to the experience** *Recollection and replay* This involves recollection and detailed unpacking of what happened in the situation about which you are thinking. | **Re-evaluating the experience** *Working with the whole experience* Here you would seek to consider all behaviours, thoughts and feelings that were involved in the experience and examine these in the light of previous experiences. This allows you to develop new insights and to test your developing knowledge. | **Integrating learning** |
|---|---|---|---|
| | *Attending to feelings* This model includes considering the feelings and emotional content of the experience as this can assist in moving your learning forward or indeed remove unhelpful barriers to reflection if you become stuck in your feelings. | *Association* Previous knowledge and experience can be used to situate and evaluate your experiences. This shows that the process is developmental and following this through your practice learning opportunity will show your progress. | *Validation* This involves putting your new insights and learning to the test to check out how it will assist your practice in future situations. It gives you a chance to modify your learning. |
| | | *Integration* New insights and prior knowledge can be integrated for future use in practice settings. | *Appropriation* Valuable learning can become part of our sense of self and part of our make-up. |

*Figure 2.3* *A model for reflective practice (after Boud et al., 1985)*

### Keeping a reflective diary or learning log

A key element of all models of reflection is to base the process on your experiences and therefore to focus on actual events or situations that you have experienced during your practice learning. A good way of beginning the process is to keep a diary or log of events that have occurred. However, rather than simply writing a historical account of what happened, it is useful to focus on the following:

- your reaction to the event or experience;

- different ways you might think about it;

- how the experience links with others you have had either prior to or during the practice learning opportunity;

- how the experience might be understood drawing on theoretical learning you have undertaken;

- what you have learned from the situation;

- what you have identified that you need to learn;

- how you might achieve your identified learning goals.

A pro forma for recording experiences in a reflective diary can be found in Figure 2.4.

**REFLECTIVE JOURNAL**

**DATE:**

Brief description of significant event

What was I feeling at the time?

How did I react and why? What was informing my decisions?

On reflection I achieved/learned ...

And I could have done differently ...

My future learning needs are ...

***Figure 2.4*** *An example of a reflective journal*

Keeping a reflective diary is not easy. On a busy practice learning experience it is often something that gets left behind or completed in a cursory way. It is not only the time factor that prevents students from completing a diary. The investment in thinking and feeling that can be demanded by the exercise may also put people off. However, systematically collecting information about experiences, thoughts and feelings about those experiences and what they mean for your learning and development is likely to contribute significantly to your supervision sessions, your overall assessment and, most important of all, to the development of best practice for those using your services in the future.

### Narratives and critical incidents

Another tool that can be used to foster reflective practice is the narrative which we briefly mentioned earlier. In many ways this is similar to keeping a reflective journal but is more in-depth and fosters a deeper level of personal engagement with the experiences and learning. Noble (2001) indicates that people resort to telling stories when they want to explain something from their own particular perspective. An important element of this is that the story reflects the voice of the tellers and, therefore, gives them a sense of control and power. This can be translated into practice learning settings by asking you to write a story or narrative about a learning experience. This has been found to be helpful in exploring how knowledge is constructed and used and can structure future learning. As part of developing the reflective process in practice learning, Noble, at the University of Western Sydney in Australia, asks students to produce narratives about their practice and learning. This individualises the learning process and can help you make sense of events that happen during your learning in a social work agency. A similar process is used within my own university and the brief for students follows:

### Story telling on practice learning (after Noble, undated)

*Describe in detail, but not more than about 500 words, a significant learning experience that took place during this week (include some examples for easy reference).*

*In telling this story position yourself as the author, and write in the first person. Include conversations with significant people involved in the experience, make links with present and past experiences, describe feelings, connect with ideas and other experiences. Look for life's meanings for those involved and the meaning of your own life at the heart of the story. Link the intellectual, spiritual, moral, social, physical and aesthetic dimensions in the telling of the story.*

Using narratives in this way is no easy task and demands a great deal of thought, insight and reflection. Done well, it can enhance your learning, but it can be painful and to use this model you will need the support of your practice teacher. Let us consider, briefly, an extract from a narrative written after your visit to the daughter whose mother had been diagnosed with dementia.

### Narrative extract

I remember feeling nervous during the visit which was strange for me as I have quite a bit of experience in working with older people and carers. I couldn't pin-point what it was that made me feel this way but felt justified when Martha (Mrs Jones's daughter) stood up from her chair, waved her finger at me and shouted that she didn't know why she had bothered calling us and that I was useless …

I came away almost ready to cry. I thought Martha was picking on me person-ally. My first thought was, 'I'll go back to the office and leave, I'm not cut out for this.' Then I started thinking, 'how would I feel?' and 'how might I react?' I thought back to the time when my uncle had died, some years ago now, and how we all as a family agreed that he wasn't properly looked after and that the doctor had been negligent in not diagnosing his cancer sooner. I can look back on this now with a smile, my uncle had not visited the doctor until his symp-toms were pronounced and nothing could have been done quicker. Perhaps Martha is feeling the same rage as I did.

Another in-depth tool, somewhat akin to the use of narratives, is the critical incident record (see Fook et al., 2000). Critical incidents can be described in a wide range of ways but they are in some way significant to the individual recounting them. You may decide, with your practice teacher, to define or limit the types of critical incident to record but need to be clear that it was important to you and your learning. In recording significant incidents, you should identify what the situation was, what you did in it and what hap-pened as a result of your actions. This should be followed by reflecting on the situation or event and the process by which it unfolded. You can expand the level of detail in which you describe the incident but this should focus on the purpose of the recording and should be agreed between yourself and your practice teacher if it is to be used within the practice learning context and shared as a piece of learning. By way of example, let us move forward to your next visit to Martha and your subsequent recording of it:

### The situation

This was my second visit to Martha. I was returning with some contact points where she could get information and to give her space to talk about the current situation. The visit was just between the two of us in her home. It lasted about an hour.

### What did I do?

I prepared for the visit by gathering leaflets from the local Alzheimer's Society and from a carers' support group held in the community hall near to Martha's house. I talked through the visit with my practice teacher.

When I arrived, I was flustered and started speaking immediately when she opened the door about what I had done in collecting leaflets and information. I did not give Martha time to speak

### *What happened?*

Two things happened early on in this meeting that I thought were significant. At the same time that I noticed I was speaking without letting Martha into the conversation, I saw that she was becoming cross but this changed when our eyes met. We both began to laugh. I apologised for speaking at a rush and she apologised for shouting during the last visit.

### *Reflections*

Why was this a critical incident for me? I was conscious that I was again quite nervous – I did not want to be shouted at again – so I was returning to something that was a little anxiety-provoking. Also, I was concerned that I did not use my own experiences and understanding in a way that might seem patronising. My main learning from this incident is to acknowledge my feelings and anxieties and to take a step back to consider the other person in the relationship.

The experience helped me to understand that humour can be a helpful device in promoting engagement with service users and this, in turn, helped me to understand that social work visits are human encounters.

## The centrality of reflection in social work practice learning

Johns (2000) has constructed a useful alliterative framework for understanding the importance of reflective practice for use in nurse education which is equally transferable to social work. His model concerns the ten Cs of reflection as follows:

| | |
|---|---|
| Commitment | Belief in self, acceptance of responsibility and openness to change |
| Contradiction | Tension between desirable and actual practice |
| Conflict | Harnessing energy of conflict to take appropriate action |
| Challenge and support | Confronting normative actions, beliefs, attitudes in non-threatening ways |
| Catharsis | Working through negative feelings |
| Creation | Moving beyond self to novel alternatives |
| Connection | Connecting new insights in the world of practice |

£22.99

| Caring | Realising desirable practice |
| Congruence | Reflection as a mirror for caring |
| Constructing personal knowledge in practice | Personal knowing and relevant theory to construct knowledge |

This description of reflective practice demonstrates that it includes personal and professional dimensions of learning and development at both internal and external levels. For instance, the emphasis on commitment and catharsis involve looking after oneself and dealing with and processing complex and difficult issues that arise in practice, while conflict, challenge and support indicate a need to move from the introspective to ways of practising and being that assist the social work process.

By agreeing and formulating ways of enhancing reflective learning during your practice experiences, you will begin to lay the foundations for a commitment to continual professional development. Learning for good practice does not end either when you complete your practice learning opportunity or when you complete your degree, but continues throughout your professional career. By fostering an openness to change and development you will be able to nurture the skills to learn after you qualify.

## C H A P T E R   S U M M A R Y

In this chapter you have explored some of the key reasons why social workers need to integrate theory and practice and considered some strategies for beginning to do so explicitly within your practice learning experience. You have been introduced to some of the complex yet important debates concerning reflection and reflective practice. Ways of using the models to enhance your learning have been included.

Practice learning begins to hone your knowledge, skills and values as a professional. It is important to remember that this learning process is continuous and what you are doing in practice now can form the basis for future learning. Thinking about the integration of theory and practice and reflection begin before practice learning in an agency starts. They do not suddenly appear. Preparation for practice learning is crucial and it is to this that we shall turn in the following chapter.

**FURTHER READING**

**Watson, F., Burrows, H. and Player, C.** (2002) Integrating Theory and Practice in Social Work Education. London: Jessica Kingsley.
This is a useful text dealing with many of the complexities of integrating theory into the practice of social work. It is written from a range of perspectives that will help you make connections.

**Gould, N. and Taylor, I.** (1996) Reflective Learning for Social Work. Aldershot: Ashgate.
This is a helpful edited collection of papers that introduce the concept of reflection and its centrality in learning for practice, and provide a range of ideas for enhancing reflective practice.

# Chapter 3
## Preparing for practice

## Introduction

The requirements for the new degree in social work (Department of Health, 2002) include a stipulation that students are assessed by their universities as fit for undertaking practice learning prior to taking up these opportunities. The responsibility of universities is to:

*Ensure that all students undergo assessed preparation for direct practice to ensure their safety to undertake practice learning in a service delivery setting. This preparation must include the opportunity to develop a greater understanding of the experience of service users and the opportunity to shadow an experienced social worker.*

*(Department of Health, 2002, p3)*

Students can take steps themselves to ensure that they are ready to maximise gains from the practice learning experience and to give their best to the learning setting and agency. Some of the ways in which you might be able to prepare for practice learning will be explored. Also in this chapter individual issues such as personal learning styles and theories of learning will be considered and you will be invited to identify issues in the learning process for yourself. There will be a chance to reflect on and identify learning needs and to set an action plan for meeting those needs.

The chapter will also consider the practical aspects of matching and selection of practice learning opportunities and pre-practice learning meetings as a central part of preparing for practice. The development, use and negotiation of a practice learning curriculum will be introduced as a way of organising your journey through practice.

# Preparation and assessment for practice learning

The responsibility for preparing and assessing you as fit for practice learning adds an important dimension to the education of social workers and emphasises the centrality of practice. There are many ways in which universities will prepare you and make an assessment of your suitability for practice. In this section, we will explore a number of ways that might be employed (see Figure 3.1).

**Figure 3.1** *Preparation and assessment for practice learning*

## Self-declarations

When you begin your social work qualifying programme, you will be required to complete a self-declaration form confirming your fitness to study for a professional qualification in social work. While this form will differ from programme to programme, it will cover two common areas: your health and any criminal convictions, bind-overs or cautions. For many programmes of social work this self-declaration form, augmented by follow-up health checks where necessary and by an enhanced Criminal Records Bureau disclosure (a comprehensive consideration of information relating to your public character), will form an integral part of your assessment as fit for practice learning.

It may seem as though this is a one-off process undertaken at the outset of your programme and, subsequently, quickly forgotten. However, it is important that you do not view it like this, but, rather, understand it as an organic process that evolves throughout your professional education and into professional practice once qualified. This is central given the GSCC's role in registration and professional regulation. Once you have qualified, you will be expected to register with the GSCC in order to practise as a social worker. Part of the assessment of your fitness to practise social work will be to consider your honesty in acknowledging issues of professional suitability and informing your employers of anything that may impact on your practice with service users. During your qualifying education, it is expected that you will begin this process and state any issues or concerns that may prevent you from practising safely.

## Personal supervision

Completing, and continually reflecting upon, your self-declaration of health and character is only one aspect of assessing your fitness to undertake practice learning. It is likely that you will have 'progress' or 'personal supervision' meetings with a tutor. (The name of these meetings may differ within each institution but the intention will be common in aiming to offer personal and academic support to you as a student.) These meetings may feed into the overall process of assessment of suitability for practice learning with your tutor offering a report or assessment of your development and fitness. If this is the case, it might be useful to use your self-declaration to structure one of these meetings, especially if there are any changes to your situation or circumstances as the following case studies indicate.

---

CASE STUDY

*Jane was a quiet, hard-working student with no health issues and a clear criminal record when she completed her self-declaration form. Her father became seriously ill during the first two months of her degree and died just four weeks before the start of her first placement. Jane thought that if she said anything to her tutor or took any time off from the programme she might jeopardise her first practice learning experience or even her career. She kept quiet. Unfortunately, dealing with vulnerable and often very upset people during her practice learning was something that became too much for Jane and she terminated the experience and subsequently left the programme.*

*Jennifer, a student on the same programme as Jane, also had no health issues or criminal convictions to declare when she completed her initial form. She experienced a breakdown in her relationship with her boyfriend before the first practice learning opportunity started and she began to have panic attacks. Jennifer was worried that she may not be able to cope with practice at this time and she informed her personal tutor of the situation. The tutor, the practice teacher in the agency where she would be based and Jennifer met to decide a way forward. It was agreed that Jennifer would take some time out from the programme, seek help to deal with her panic attacks and complete her practice learning, in the same agency, at a later date. While this extended her programme and was difficult financially, she was able to complete her degree successfully. Her declaration and action was considered to represent a positive strength and a professional way of managing her situation.*

---

## Shadowing a qualified social worker

You will have the opportunity to 'shadow' a qualified and experienced social worker prior to undertaking practice learning. This means that you will be expected to spend time alongside a social worker in his or her daily activities. This is important in preparing you for the world of practice. It can provide you with a valuable experience of what social workers do in a particular agency and how they do it. There are issues of confidentiality and professional protocol that will need to be explicitly considered in undertaking this activity and your programme should be able to guide you with these.

Some programmes will ask you to gain this experience prior to beginning your studies and to bring evidence to demonstrate you have completed the task, while other programmes will include time during your studies for you to achieve this. Whichever way you have been asked to complete the task of shadowing a social worker, you should aim to gain the maximum possible learning from the experience. This is also the case given that programmes will require you to spend different lengths of time undertaking this activity. If you have worked in a particular social care agency prior to your studies, it might be useful to arrange to spend time in a different social care environment serving different service users. Sometimes the unfamiliar helps one to focus, to observe more keenly and to question more closely an experience. It is always helpful to reflect on the experience (see Chapter 2). Asking yourself the following questions and recording as fully as possible your experiences will help to develop a reflective approach to your learning.

---

### *A reflective critique of the shadowing experience*

- *What situations did I observe and in what settings did they occur?*

- *What did I learn from the experience?*

- *How might it have been different in another setting?*

- *What do I need to learn more about?*

- *How might I go about learning more?*

---

Of course, your programme will, no doubt, have provided you with a pro forma set of questions about your shadowing experience. The importance of shadowing for assessing your fitness for practice learning is twofold. Firstly, the evidence from the social worker will assist your programme in determining your readiness and, secondly, your reflections and recordings also demonstrate your suitability or otherwise at this point.

## Academic preparation and the experiences of service users

Preparation for practice is likely to involve assessment of some of the academic modules you are studying. Each programme, again, will have different course components and criteria for assessing preparation for practice, but interpersonal skills modules and theory and methods modules directly concern the practice application of knowledge and may constitute part of your assessment (see Research Summary 3.1).

Teaching and learning experiences concerning service users are also central to the preparation of practice. On some programmes it may be the case that service users have a direct input into practice preparation and your assessment. On others, it is your knowledge of the experience of service users that will be considered. The importance of knowledge of service user experiences cannot be underestimated as your practice learning will have an impact on the lives of people using your services and the agencies in which you are placed. However, it is important to remember that individual service users and carers are the experts on their unique situations, thoughts and feelings. This needs to be at the forefront of your learning about service user experiences to guard against treating everyone in the same way regardless of experience.

*Leveridge (2003) reported on the development of a module designed to ensure that the levels and skills of social work students was at an appropriate level for their first practice learning experience. This work anticipated much of what is now required as preparation for practice learning in the qualifying social work degree.*

*Preparation and assessment for undertaking practice learning is multi-faceted (see Figure 3.1, p39). It is fundamental to your learning and professional development and you should seek to maximise what use you make of it as this is likely to add to a positive assessment. The emphasis was on 'learning' as preparation or practice rather than being taught. This offers students a more active role in engaging with the subject at a deep level and working with issues that have a direct bearing on practice learning.*

*Maidment's (2003) research in Australia also has a bearing on what students need to know to be prepared for practice. She questions the adequacy of preparation and suggests, on the basis of her research, that social work programmes also need to teach students how to survive and negotiate in workplace cultures and not only the traditional interview and assessment skills. Maidment sent a 58-item questionnaire to 48 third-year students and 41 fourth-year students to complete at the end of their field placement with a 48 per cent and 39 per cent response rate respectively. The questionnaire covered demographic information, placement allocation and communication, teaching and learning, and agency context. In the results, Maidment found that 31 per cent of respondents reported verbal abuse from clients, 28 per cent travelled long distances, 38 per cent experienced conflict within the agency and 62 per cent experienced considerable work-based stress (using subjective perceptions). This suggests that health and safety and stress preparation is essential for students undertaking practice learning.*

# Adult learning and personal learning styles

Paying attention to the ways in which you learn best will help you to structure your practice learning experiences in ways that maximise your learning. As adults, we develop preferred ways of learning that derive from our experiences, who we are and what our goals might be. It is important to have an understanding of some of the ways in which adults learn and to match ourselves with styles that suit us best. In this section, we will consider models and styles of learning and examine how these link with learning in social work.

## Adult learning

The stages involved in adult learning are broadly agreed upon. Adult learning theory, or the principles associated with learning, acknowledges that adults are mature and able to identify their own learning needs and to integrate new learning into their everyday lives (Sawdon, 1986). Previous individual learning experiences are valued and used as a base on which to build (Ledbetter, 1989). The factors which have been found to be most influential in facilitating effective learning by adults are:

- *the meaningfulness of the material to be learned* – the more meaningful it appears to be in relation to the student's aspirations, the better the learning;

- *currency of practice* – when skills and knowledge are applied soon after the time of first learning, there appears to be better recall at a later date;

- *performance anxiety* – the effects are greater for adults rather than children in respect of self-esteem and self-confidence;

- *speed of performance* – adults operate best when they set the pace;

- *perceived relevance* – adults need to be able to judge and question the relevance of learning.

So, the point to be made here is that the more you find your learning relevant and linked to your goal of becoming a social worker the more likely you are to learn. Practice learning opportunities allow you to apply the knowledge and, if this is undertaken in a safe and reasonably protective environment, it may enhance effective learning. Certainly, considering the factors involved in adult learning, it seems that practice learning offers you valuable ways of developing. One thing to remember, however, is that you will have your own preferred pace of learning. While practice learning does not present an environment that can always be fully managed, and part of your learning will be to find ways of dealing with the unexpected and the immediate, it is important that you share your preferred pace of learning with your practice teacher as part of your preparation for practice.

The work of Knowles (1984, 1990) has been influential in understanding adult learning. He outlined four basic assumptions involved in adult learning as follows:

1. Positive changes occur in the adult's self-concept as the individual matures. People move from total dependency on teachers and learning by rote to increasing self-directedness.

2. As individuals mature, they accumulate experiences which represent a rich resource for future learning. An individual's experiences define the identity of the person and, therefore, need to be acknowledged and, indeed, used to assess current situations and future learning needs.

3. There is an increasing readiness to learn in adults which is a function of developmental tasks required for the performance of evolving social roles.

4. The orientation to learning becomes problem-centred rather than subject-centred.

Motivation is, of course an important factor in successful learning and it might suggested that adult learners will fare best in situations which allow them to:

- experience a degree of self-determination and choice in relation to what they learn and how they learn it; and

- feel that the activities they are engaging in are increasing their competence in areas that they have defined by themselves through the skilled insertion of opportunities for informational feedback (see Vroom and Deci, 1992).

If the above points will help your motivation, an important way in which you can be involved in structuring your practice learning experience is to consult with your practice teacher and negotiate a learning plan to guide you through it.

Despite the importance of Knowles's work, however, it has not escaped criticism and there is little empirical evidence to support the principles he has outlined (Fry et al., 2003). He omits reference to social characteristics and ignores political, gender and race issues that may influence opportunities for learning and approaches to learning resulting from these factors (Humphries, 1988). Despite this, the principles of adult learning are important and influential, but, as Humphries (1988) suggests, they need to be placed within a clear value base that acknowledges the relationship between social divisions and access to educational opportunities.

## Learning in social work

Learning to develop practice skills and competence in social work is a highly complex process. A number of models have been developed to help explain the learning process. In practice the models intertwine and overlap. The main ones are included below.

---

### *Theories of learning*

#### *Behavioural theories*

*In these the teacher is central to the process. Although it is generally associated with skills-focused teaching, it is not limited to this domain. Cognitive and attitudinal learning, or ways in which you might think about a situation, may also result. Modelling, feedback and positive reinforcement are critical to success.*

*An example of behavioural learning may be seen in being asked to write a letter to a service user to arrange a visit. It can help to be shown the agency style and some examples and to receive feedback on your effort so you can adapt your letter writing in the future. You may gain positive reinforcement from the feedback or the praise of your practice teacher or you may be able to gain satisfaction from the fact that the letter was posted, showing that it was written to an appropriate standard.*

#### *Cognitive theories*

*These describe some of the ways in which concepts and knowledge are acquired. Information should be presented in such a way as to make links with prior learning, to progress in cumulative steps and to have appropriate goals and self-assessments to guide future learning. Cognitive learning concepts suggest that new information will be more quickly and effectively assimilated if an overall framework is presented consisting of the most general and inclusive ideas. (This can be achieved by a clear framework and guidelines outlining the practice curriculum to be used during practice learning.)*

*One useful example of cognitive learning concerns the production of a pen picture describing your route into social work and using this to focus discussion with your practice teacher. It will help you make links with your prior experiences and the social work role and tasks that you can integrate into a clear developmental plan for learning. Even if you do not think that your practice teacher will want to see a pen picture it can be a useful exercise to undertake.*

---

*Humanist theories*

*These are appropriate when learning to learn and in learning situations involving a substantial affective component (Rogers, 1967). Learners share experiences, examine ideas and beliefs and draw out conclusions from the learning processes in which they have been involved. Learning is very much self-directed.*

*As a way of preparing for practice and supporting your learning, it can be help-ful to form a peer or study group among other students undertaking practice learning at the same time. You can meet or share experiences online as a way of dealing with some of the emotions that arise during practice learning. Of course, you must ensure that such a group operates within the confidentiality procedures required by your programme and agency, but there is great poten-tial for learning and support here.*

*In higher education terms, this way of using experiential learning and work relates to the use of action learning sets. These allow students to learn about themselves and the project in which they are involved by reflection on what they are doing:*

> *Action learning is thus based on the idea that effective learning and development come from working through real-life problems with people. As a support for experiential learning it stresses the dual importance of understanding and action.*
> *(Beatty, 2003, p142)*

It is a combination of all three models of learning described above that maximises oppor-tunities for successful practice learning. Learning is not about adding knowledge to a person but about the person being actively engaged in constructing learning from these domains by integrating it with and extending past experiences (Biggs and Moore, 1993).

Gardiner (1989) found a close relationship between approaches to learning and the out-come of the learning. Approaches to learning can be influenced by the perceptions you might have of what is required of you in your learning, the nature and form of teaching and assessment, and the context of learning. Using Scandinavian research that identified 'surface approaches' that are reproductive and passive, and 'deep approaches' that are characterised by the search for meaning and are active and constructive, Gardiner found that outcomes were more favourable in students who sought meaning and attempted to integrate learning into practice experiences. This accords with the principles of adult learn-ing that emphasise the adult learner's control over their own learning and active involvement within it. This active and boundless searching for meaning and interpretation is emphasised by Howe (1996).

This model of approaches to learning has been developed further by Ramsden (2003) for higher education. It can be used to examine approaches to practice learning in social work (see Figure 3.2).

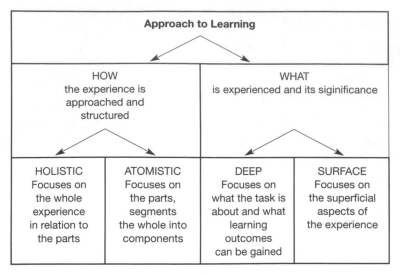

***Figure 3.2*** *Approaches to learning (adapted from Ramsden, 2003, p44)*

The following case study provides a brief example of two students' approach to learning.

*Ahmed and Michael were undertaking practice learning together in a mental health team. They were both asked to accompany a social worker to an assessment visit, after gaining permission from the service user Mark. Ahmed focused on the ways in which assessments were used in the agency, what the process would involve and how it fitted into the larger picture of Mark's involvement in the agency. He was concerned to explore the process of assessment and what it might mean for Mark, what it said about the agency and what message might be conveyed in the process. His approach to the experience was deep and holistic. Michael, on the other hand, understood the experience in terms of it being simply an assessment, which is what he saw the agency doing, and he wanted to learn what an assessment comprised and how to undertake one. His learning was, at this stage, less deep than Ahmed's, although he fluctuated between deep and surface approaches.*

Part of the role of the practice teacher is to identify, develop and provide a range of learning opportunities for students and to encourage them to observe, describe and analyse good social work practice. This involves helping students to evaluate their own learning, development and competence, and includes facilitating the integration of theory and practice, the transfer of learning, and anti-racist and anti-discriminatory practice. However, you also have a role here. It is important to identify in very honest terms what you want to get out of your practice learning opportunities and to take this to the experience and share it with your practice teacher. It will help you to consider what preferences you have for experiences and for learning and how these might impact on your learning in either 'surface' or 'deep' ways.

# Theories of learning and work-based approaches

The particular theory of learning ascribed to is important to the ways in which effectiveness is judged by the various people involved in practice learning in social work. In higher education there has been a long history of experiential learning, which, as Beatty (2003, p135) suggests 'requires a complex interweaving of knowledge, technical skills and application of professional ethics'. The Dearing Report (1997, p15) was clear in its statement that '(t)he strongest single message we received from employers was the value of work experience.' Indeed, one of the reasons why practice is deemed necessary in social work education is because employers want to see social workers who are fit for purpose, able to do the job and therefore safe, able to work collaboratively, within the appropriate legal framework in a competent, skilled and knowledgeable manner and able to account for their continued learning needs.

According to Gray (2001 – see also Ebbutt, 1996) work-based learning has four aims and types:

- as a mode of access to study or as accelerated access;

- as initial professional preparation;

- as a general preparation for the world of work;

- as a major constituent of a programme of study.

Practice learning in social work certainly accords with the last three types identified. For Gray, however, work-based learning is more than the simple acquisition of skills but is essentially centred around reflection as reviewing and learning from experience (see Chapter 2). It is based on the assumption that learning arises from action and problem-solving in the work environment and sees knowledge as a shared or collective activity. It is the acquisition of a meta-competence – which simply means learning to learn. This is central to continuing professional development and to social work practice. While universities have at times disparaged work-based learning and suggested that it lacks credibility, Gray states that there is no a priori reason to consider that it is ineffective and action learning can lead to a search for theoretical understanding. The development of experiential learning in universities has been tense; while learning in the natural world is situational and context-dependent, pure academic learning is intentional and represents a second-order experience of the world, something extrapolated from the world and theorised. Beatty (2003, p136) stated:

> The key to effective learning is the support given to the student to draw out learning from the experience and in linking critical incidents in the experience to ideas and theories which shed light on them.

Cartney's (2000) plea to focus on learning and teaching strategies that promote student learning is important and she suggests that adult learning styles, while considered important, have been little tested in a rigorous way. You have, therefore, a central role to play in your own learning as you will know best how you approach learning tasks. It is important to share this with your practice teacher so you can both identify effective strategies for learning.

Competence, comprising the integration of knowledge, skills and values, has become a watchword in social work education (CCETSW, 1996). Illeris (2003) adds that it also involves personal qualities and the ability to perform adequately and flexibly in well-known and unknown situations. For Illeris there are two fundamental assumptions concerning learning:

1. All learning includes two essentially different types of process – the external interaction between learner and social, cultural and material environment, and the internal psychological process of acquisition and elaboration in which new impulses are connected with the results of prior experience and learning.

2. All learning includes three dimensions, the cognitive (knowledge and skills), the emotional (feelings and motivation) and the social (communication and cooperation). These are all embedded within a societally situated context.

If indeed this is the case then practice learning is the key forum for learning for social workers. Students are able to interact with the complexities of the work environment and reflect on these and test their experiences against prior classroom learning. This demands bringing into play the range of human characteristics and, importantly in social work, concerns the use of a reflection on values. Figure 3.3 shows the development from knowledge acquisition to active learning and reflection.

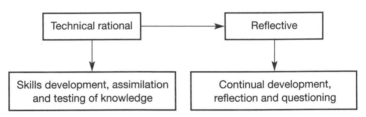

**Figure 3.3** *Knowledge acquisition to reflective learning*

---

*ACTIVITY 3.1*

*Spend some time considering knowledge and learning acquired during your programme. Identify what worked best in your learning and write this down. Then consider how you as an individual actively pursue knowledge and learning, how you set about this, what works well for you and what is not effective in assisting your learning.*

*These reflections will be important in determining your style and preferences in learning to which we will now turn. Be prepared to share your thoughts about style and preference in learning with your practice teacher.*

---

## Personal learning styles

Learning styles are seen as one part of the teaching process, drawing on the concept that in learning styles cognition, conceptualisation, affect and behaviour are interrelated. The ability to recognise different styles can help practice teachers to 'start where the student is' and therefore to design individual programmes of learning. By identifying your own preferred style of learning you will be able to be fully involved in this process and seek experiences that will maximise your learning. The use of learning styles questionnaires may help but again more work needs to be done on assessing their usefulness.

Learning styles questionnaires are often used to determine whether a student learns best by reflection, action, theorising or being led. These questionnaires are limited and if applied too rigidly might suggest to someone that this is the way they learn and that this cannot be changed. However, used with caution they may indicate preferences and help in identifying experiences and opportunities for learning. The most frequently used approach in social work is the learning styles questionnaire designed by Honey and Mumford (1982).

The learning styles of students and practice teachers may, of course, not match and the potential impact of matching or mismatching has not been explored. The impact of the institutional context on learning has also not been fully explored and it may be that learning styles are malleable and fluid rather than fixed entities (Boud and Walker, 1998).

Cartney (2000) reports on a small qualitative study exploring knowledge of learning styles as a way of promoting student learning in practice. She uses Honey and Mumford's learning styles questionnaire (LSQ) that builds on the work of Kolb. The LSQ aims to identify how people have learned in the past and how they may best learn in the future – tests of the questionnaire have mainly been conducted on white male managers, however. The impact of the socio-cultural context is accepted by Cartney who sees learning styles as one possible factor in the learning process. In Cartney's study four themes emerged:

1. Respondents found the LSQ useful in making connections between teaching and learning. Students spoke positively about potential usefulness as an aid to learning but would have liked practice teachers to have been more proactive in their use of the information.

2. On analysis of the impact of learning styles on teaching styles, practice teachers identified that they often used their own learning styles to teach rather than focusing on the style in which students preferred to learn.

3. With regard to perceptions of the effect of similarities and differences in learning styles, where there were similar styles this was perceived as positive. Students, however, pointed out that other styles might have been beneficial in promoting growth.

4. It seemed to highlight the anxieties of moving from practitioner to teacher.

Personal learning styles and a knowledge of the principles of adult learning are integral to the effective accomplishment of learning goals in the context of practice teaching and they can help in the matching process undertaken prior to practice learning.

# Matching and negotiating the practice learning experience

There remains considerable debate about how best to match student social workers with practice teachers and assessors. For instance, is it helpful to place people together who have a similar approach to social work and a similar style of personal development and learning? Or, on the other hand, is it better for a student social worker to be taught and assessed in practice by someone who has a different approach so that this might stretch and challenge the student in considering and testing novel and alternative approaches to social work practice and learning? In her study, Cartney (2000) raised some of these questions. She completed semi-structured interviews with practice teachers and students, finding that those sharing similar learning styles saw this as positive and no practice teacher referred to similarities in learning styles as problematic. Student social workers were in general agreement but did identify that where there were differences in learning style this had the potential to promote growth and development. It was not felt that differences in learning styles adversely affected the practice learning experience. Differences were only perceived as problematic in the context of difficulties arising within the student and practice teacher relationship. It is likely, therefore, that you will be able to use your personal learning style in a positive way and sharing this at the outset with your practice teachers will be beneficial, whether or not you share a similar approach to learning. However, in matching for the practice learning experience the fostering of a positive working and learning relationship will be more important.

Your university will play a large role in organising your practice learning opportunity and will be involved in the matching process. You have a key role in developing the practice learning arrangements and, to gain the most out of the experience, you need to engage with the process as fully as possible.

## The application process

Matching begins when you are asked to set out your areas of interest and/or apply for a practice learning experience. While the processes of organising and arranging practice learning will differ from university to university, there are common elements to each. One way of beginning the process concerns the completion of an application form. This is likely to include information about any previous work – voluntary or paid – that you may have undertaken, your particular interests in social work and the area in which you wish to undertaken practice learning. The level of study you are at and which practice learning experience you are applying for (first, second, third and so on) will also be important, as will the academic work you have completed on the programme so far. You are also likely to be asked about your personal circumstances and needs as they might influence your practice learning work. From this information, your university will work with practice agencies to identify possible practice learning opportunities that meet your needs as a student of social work. It is fundamental that you complete any such requests as fully as possible. Indeed, it is worthwhile considering this in the same terms as a job application and spend time getting it right. If in doubt, ask your friends and colleagues to comment or your university tutor. An example of a completed form is included below.

# Practice Learning Request Form

All sections of this form must be completed in full. Failure to do so may delay the practice learning identification process.

| | |
|---|---|
| **Name:** | James Freeman |
| **Contact address:** | 1 The Garth<br>Sandtown<br>SD1 1SD |
| **Telephone number:** | 0012 345 678 |
| **Mobile number:** | 00987 654321 |
| **E-mail address** | **JF@Sandtown.net** |
| **My specialist area of interest is:** e.g. adults, children and families, mental health, learning disability, substance use, other. (Please note you are not guaranteed a practice learning opportunity in your area of interest.) | Older people with dementia |
| **Your expectations of the practice learning:** | I am hoping to gain experience of working in a multi-disciplinary team and to be involved in making assessments of need, planning and coordinating services for people with dementia and their carers. If I cannot have a practice learning experience within dementia setting, I hope I can work with a range of other professionals undertaking the tasks I've mentioned, which I believe can be transferred to other settings. |
| **Your perceived learning needs:** | I need to gain confidence in using the telephone.<br>I want to increase my knowledge of working with people directly.<br>I need to develop an understanding of how theory can be applied to practice.<br>I need to learn how to compile reports that are not too long but say everything that needs to be said. |

| What modules have you taken so far? | Introduction to social work practice and theory<br>Social policy and sociology for social workers<br>Law for social workers<br>Working with adults<br>Psychology for social workers<br>Communication skills |
|---|---|
| **Core Information** ||
| **Academic supervisor and contact:** | Jane Doe<br>**doej@university.ac.uk** |
| **Your educational qualifications:** | GCSE Mathematics C<br>GCSE English B<br>GCSE French C<br>GCSE History B<br>GSCE Technology and Design D<br><br>A level French B<br>A level English D<br>NVQ Level 2 Health and social care |
| **Work experience<br>(paid and voluntary):** | I work as a care worker in a residential care home at weekends and took my NVQ here.<br>I worked in a special school for young people with learning disabilities as part of my work experience at school. |
| **Significant factors to take into account during practice learning, e.g. family care-giving responsibilities, disability** | None |
| **Do you have transport?** | No |
| **In support of your application** ||
| **(Please tell us, in no more than 300 words, what you expect to gain from this practice learning experience and what skills, knowledge and personal qualities you will bring to practice learning)** ||
| I hope to increase my knowledge of people with dementia and to understand better their needs. I hope to work with people with dementia and their carers once I qualify and believe that I will gain from understanding the assessment ||

and planning process and working with other professionals. I am happy to consider a practice learning opportunity with any service user group or field of practice in which I can gain this experience.

I have developed a friendly and approachable manner during my work at Greens Residential Home. I am able to get along with colleagues and the people I work with in the home and believe this would be an asset to any practice learning opportunity. My developing knowledge about social work will be enhanced during practice learning and I am hopeful that I can take my knowledge from modules into this setting.

I am a fast and willing learner, prepared to try my hand at anything and I believe I will be able to make a valuable contribution to the agency in which I undertake my practice learning while gaining a lot from there for my future career.

**Signed:**

**Date:**

---

### ACTIVITY 3.2

*Using the form above, construct your own request for a practice learning opportunity. Identify priority issues and what you think is important in matching. Consider why you have chosen these aspects and how you might work with an alternative experience.*

*You may have suggested that it is important for you to have a specific opportunity because of your interests or because you have worked in other areas. Your university may suggest a different agency, however, and focus on learning needs and the standards you are required to meet. It is important to think clearly about what you need and why you need it. The social work degree is generic and while universities will want to match you appropriately, their concerns will be centred on the appropriateness and adequacy of the learning environment.*

You may not hear about your practice learning opportunity for some time, depending on how your programme organises its practice learning. You should seek clarity about the process to allay any anxieties that may arise while you are waiting.

## First contact and the learning agreement

Once the practice learning opportunity is arranged and your practice teacher or assessor has been identified it is good practice for you to meet so that you may begin to establish what your role will be, what your learning needs are and how these may be met within this practice learning context. You should be proactive in seeking a meeting as this will help you develop skills as a learner with some responsibility for creating and developing experiences in practice. It is the pre-practice learning opportunity meeting that can be useful in addressing differences in style and personality and help you to identify and work out strategies for dealing effectively with these. Your practice teacher will want to match you with opportunities and experiences that will assist you in meeting the requirements of your programme, the National Occupational Standards and your own personal identified learning needs. The following case study offers an example of a first meeting.

---

**CASE STUDY**

*Petra wanted a practice learning opportunity in a fostering team as she had a particular interest in substitute care. It had not been possible to arrange such an experience but she had been offered a practice learning opportunity in a voluntary childcare team. At first she was disappointed but, prior to meeting her practice teacher, she thought about and wrote down what she was interested in learning, why this was so and how she thought she approached her learning. She made some notes about what she wanted to gain from the experience and added a pen picture that described her move to the UK from Croatia some ten years previously. She took these notes to her meeting with her practice teacher who was grateful to use them as a way of structuring the meeting. It transpired that there were a number of young people in the agency who were in the 'looked after' system and that she would be able to work with them. Also, she was asked if she would help with a recently formed group for unaccompanied children. Petra felt that her needs were being attended to and that she had contributed to the matching process.*

---

Each programme will have its own way of assessing and collecting evidence for practice learning (see Chapter 5). It is likely that you will have a learning agreement that details what you will be expected to achieve and experience. Some of these outcomes will be specified and non-negotiable but some may be negotiated by yourself and your practice teacher or assessor and other interested parties. Where negotiation is possible you should use the initial organisational process and matching to delineate your needs and expectations. This helps in preventing disappointment at the outset over the practice learning opportunity and allows both yourself and the agency to be clear about what can be offered and so further assists the matching process.

The practice learning agreement is an important component of the learning process. It will set out what you have to achieve in order to meet the standards and requirements for successful practice learning and will, no doubt, link to the agency's practice curriculum, if they have one. You should familiarise yourself with the non-negotiable components of the agreement, and consider carefully what you would hope to include in the negotiated part. The following example shows part of Petra's individualised learning agreement with the Blueskies Childcare Team. The non-negotiable elements are not included.

As can be seen from the short extract from Petra's learning agreement she was able to negotiate specific aspects of the experience that met her initial preferences. This is not always the case, of course. The important issue is to ensure that whatever experiences you are engaged in you are meeting the standards and requirements needed to qualify as a social worker.

---

**CASE STUDY** *continued*

*Petra's learning agreement:*

**Practical arrangements**
*Days per week on placement: Five*
*Agreed study time:*     *Half a day per week*
*Expected hours of work:*     *8.30 am to 5 pm, 4.30 pm on Fridays*
*University contact days:*     *To be arranged*

**Outline of proposed workload:**
*(what quantity and range of tasks will the student be involved in)*

*Petra will carry a caseload of between five and ten young people.*

*She will be involved in assessment work, case planning and direct work, including play work.*

*Petra will work with the behaviour management team with the foster care group.*

*Petra will work with the 'I'm not alone' group, designing sessions and evaluating them.*

*Petra will make contact with the local authority foster care team and arrange to spend a day with them.*

*Petra will attend at least one case conference during her practice learning opportunity.*

*Petra will arrange to spend a day in court with one of the social workers.*

---

# The practice learning curriculum: developing a personal learning plan in the agency context

## What is a practice curriculum?

While you are likely to have begun your practice learning opportunity when you come to consider using a practice curriculum to assist your learning, it can still be thought of legitimately as preparation for practice. A practice curriculum, in simple terms, is a systematic collection of learning opportunities and experiences designed to meet the demands and needs of a range of stakeholders involved in work-based learning. These may include:

- national education and training bodies;

- the local educational institution; and

- each individual student (Shardlow and Doel, 1996).

In some ways all practice learning opportunities are based around a higher order practice curriculum. The main elements constituting a practice curriculum are the key learning opportunities and issues that will be covered by all students undertaking practice learning within that agency, consortium or university, depending on who designs and implements it. In respect of social work, these relate to the prescribed areas of knowledge, skills and values set by the Department of Health (2002), the GSCC (2002), the National Occupational Standards (TopssEngland, 2003) and the subject benchmarking criteria. However, individual agencies or practice teachers may develop activities and learning opportunities to meet prescribed and negotiated needs. A good practice curriculum aims to do this in a flexible way that accounts for individual and particular needs and will build on the learning agreement for practice learning.

As we have seen in our consideration of adult learning, students start at different stages of development in their learning. Some may have many years as health or social care practitioners in a range of fields. Such experienced students often present a challenge to practice teachers and other agency staff because of their wide range of knowledge and skills. Others entering qualifying education have very little professional experience. It is an important task for you to identify learning goals and needs with your practice teacher and to prepare a unique learning and development plan that covers the required areas to be included in the curriculum, and individual needs which are negotiated and included in individual learning agreements. Used in this way a practice curriculum will provide a useful tool in guiding successful experimentation in practice (see below).

## The practice curriculum

A practice curriculum structures students' learning in practice. It is much more than simply the specification of teaching content, although it does include a clear statement of what will be taught. Shardlow and Doel (1996) employ a sequential or 'building-block' approach to the practice curriculum. The competency-based approach to social work education does not provide a curriculum in itself and they suggest that the practice teacher must respond flexibly to the learning needs of students. Indeed, the Department of Health decided not to prescribe the curriculum for social work education and so each university and agency is able to design a practice curriculum that will encourage attainment of core knowledge and skills within a particular environment. Important steps in designing a practice curriculum include:

- defining the aims of the curriculum;
- identifying the content;
- considering the merits of sequence;
- devising the methods and strategies of learning;
- considering issues of measurement of learning;
- presenting the material in accessible form;
- reviewing and evaluating the curriculum;
- writing the final version.

Practice learning agreements generally detail the requirements of practice learning for the social work degree and the standards and units to be achieved. Learning agreements set out the specific learning opportunities available within the agency and the expectations to be covered by all student social workers. There is potential, as we have seen, to negotiate individual objectives at the outset and these form part of the overall assessment process.

Thus, in practice, there is a line moving from a rigid and prescribed curriculum to a more flexible and individual one. The most rigid part of the practice curriculum stems from the National Occupation Standards, the Department of Health requirements and the subject benchmarks underpinning the degree. While the requirements outlined are fixed and non-negotiable, they can be presented in such a way that agencies can make them specific to their particular work. It is, however, in the negotiated components that flexibility and uniqueness form part of the learning process. It is at this more specific level that particular agency opportunities are likely to be specified and where you can introduce your learning needs and objectives. Indeed, if the agency does not use a practice curriculum, it is worth using the negotiated part of the practice learning agreement to construct one for yourself. If this is done close to the outset of your practice learning experience it will form a useful structure and focus for the experience.

# A practice curriculum model

In this section, you are introduced to an example of a practice curriculum that includes some of the tasks and opportunities that might be involved. You can adapt these to meet your learning needs in the light of a negotiated practice learning agreement.

## Aims

There are four main aims running through the practice curriculum as a whole. These are:

- to develop core knowledge and skills;
- to foster a critically reflective approach to practice;
- to develop a sense of self-responsibility for learning;
- to identify learning needs and plan how these can be met.

The practice learning opportunity represents the point at which you begin to apply your learning and is often approached with longing and expectation, but tempered with apprehension and anxiety. An induction, which forms the first part of the practice curriculum, can provide focus and structure to allay some of these anxieties. A practice curriculum can be separated broadly into two sections: the induction and the continuing curriculum. This is not fixed and, in practice, the two sections overlap and merge. They are separated here for ease of explanation.

## Induction

The induction activities deal with such matters as working within organisations, developing professional competence and learning – by discussion, observation and active participation. The activities concern forming relationships with service users and planning with them to meet needs. There is an emphasis on evaluation and reflection in practice.

The practice curriculum introduces you to a series of activities that are designed to develop a working knowledge of the area, the services and the resources of the agency and its workings and philosophies. The activities are undertaken individually and in small groups and are backed up with regular and frequent supervision (see Chapter 4). This helps to ensure that your learning needs are taken into account and learning opportunities and experiences are matched with them.

The activities contained in an induction may include some of the following:

1. A group exercise aimed at identifying expectations, anxieties and hopes for the students while on practice learning as an ice-breaker.

2. An individual activity drawing a pen picture of yourself and your reasons for entering social work education. This is not easy and the activity can evoke painful memories that you may need to deal with.

3. The compilation of a list of strengths and needs, which may be undertaken individually, and the development of an individual student action plan designed to begin to meet identified needs or to determine ways in which these might be met (an example of these activities is shown below).

4. A group activity designed to increase knowledge and awareness of the resources and services provided locally.

5. The organisation of a series of visits to local agencies of particular interest to the practice agency, individual or small groups of students.

6. The final activity covering the induction period could be the negotiation of the practice learning agreement, including negotiable and non-negotiable elements.

---

### ACTION AND LEARNING PLANS

*Some students find it useful to include a systematic learning plan as part of their practice learning opportunity. To help develop this way of recording and keeping track of your learning, a plan is included below. This can be adapted to suit individual styles of learning.*

#### My list of strengths

*(Consider here anything that you consider yourself to be good at, including personal qualities, practical tasks and more abstract qualities. List as many as you can and don't be modest!)*

#### My list of needs

*(Here you should include experiences, practice skills, knowledge, learning and core qualities that you feel you need to increase, develop or introduce into your repertoire of skills and behaviour. Again, as with the list of strengths, it is important to be honest in order for you to judge your progress throughout the practice learning opportunity.)*

*ACTION PLAN*
*Need identified:*

*Resources needed to meet need:*

*(It may be useful to list the practical resources, the learning and knowledge resources, the skills base and the personal resources in such an order or to take a thematic approach listing resources of a particular type.)*

*List methods by which resources can be gained:*

*(At this point you should begin to work out an action plan within the plan to gain access to resources, i.e. if you need to acquaint yourself more fully with a particular aspect of the case you may need time to spend researching this in the library, or you may need to speak with a relevant authority, or attend a workshop or lecture.)*

*What do you need from your practice teacher?*

*What do you need from colleagues?*

*Methods by which you will evaluate your learning:*

*(List some of the ways in which you will check out that you are meeting your learning needs. This may include discussion and feedback from colleagues, clients and practice teacher. It may include self-reporting in relation to confidence. It may involve presenting your learning to colleagues for critical review.)*

*The action plan:*

*(Write down a series of steps and stages that are involved in the meeting of your identified learning needs.)*

The function of this induction period is to allow you to gradually attune to the new expectations and demands of practice linking your experiences from the academic arena. It assists in promoting focus on the practice learning component of education in which the integration of academic knowledge and practice skills is emphasised. It also provides a period of reflection during which you may begin to identify individual learning needs and goals. Relevant learning objectives and a structured and individually paced introduction to learning can help in increasing motivation. The other important function of the induction period is to serve as an orientation to personnel in your agency and external agencies in the locality. Thus the induction can be said to provide:

• consolidation – of past experiences and prior learning;

• reflection – on new and old learning and experiences;

• orientation – to professional practice;

• the basis for action – for future professional development.

## Continuing curriculum

The continuing curriculum may then consider more agency-specific aspects of learning or the development of advanced skills in practice. An example of a possible curriculum element follows.

---

### *PRACTICE SKILLS PAIRS*

*Most students are apprehensive of the first time they knock on the door of a family home and of how they will conduct an interview. To give you some practice in this essential skill, we therefore require you to undertake an interview role-play with another student and to have this recorded on video. There are video facilities at Agency House. The room requires prior booking as it is also used for other purposes. Please check in the diary (located in the secretary's office) to see when the room is available.*

*You are provided with four scenarios to work from (see below). You can take it in turn with your partner to interview and be interviewed using these scenarios. Both roles are valuable for learning. It is also important to learn how to operate the video-recording facility. Many students have found it useful to use this 'for real' with individuals or families with whom they are working. Permission to record an interview on audio or videotape must be obtained from those concerned. We have a form to complete for this purpose (see your practice teacher).*

*An interview checklist is provided so that you can prepare a framework and be aware of the aspects of the interview which are important. This checklist or something similar will be used by your practice teacher when observing your practice. It is a requirement of the placement that students' work with service users should be directly observed on at least three occasions. You will learn a lot by watching the video with your student partner and you should also take the opportunity of watching it with your practice teacher within a supervision sessions, so that you can check out your perceptions of how you did. Experience has often shown that students are very hard on themselves!*

*You should produce a short critical analysis of your skills and presentation (about one side of A4 will suffice).*

***Practice Skills Pairs***

***Aim:*** *To undertake a video-recorded interview with a student colleague.*

***Learning outcomes:***

- *To develop, practise and enhance your interpersonal skills and interviewing techniques in a safe environment.*

- *To evaluate critically and to reflect upon your own practice.*

- *To increase learning opportunities and share experiences with student colleagues.*

- *To identify learning needs and begin to develop your skills as a reflective practitioner.*

*Method:*

- *Read information concerning interpersonal skills.*

- *Choose a case from the examples below.*

- *In the case you choose you are the client. Your colleague will interview you concerning the issues presented.*

- *Spend about 20–30 minutes on each interview.*

- *Each interview should be video-recorded.*

- *Following each interview discuss between yourselves how you felt the interview progressed.*

- *Watch the video and identify what skills were employed, what you were pleased with and what areas of learning you need to account for.*

- *In supervision with your practice teacher bring your video, thoughts and reflection for discussion.*

*Case scenarios:*

(a) *You are a young parent living on a new estate in a large village. You have recently moved there and know few people. You have one child at the local primary school, and two children at home. You work part-time three evenings each week in a local pub while your partner looks after the children. You have become concerned that your eldest child is saying that the other children do not like her, hit her and call her names. Recently she has become very distressed at going to school and is refusing to go. Until this you believe she has been a happy, friendly child. You do not know what to do and have decided to visit a community advice worker recommended by a schoolteacher.*

(b) *You have a large outstanding debt with both the electricity company and gas company - £485 and £654 respectively. You are also behind with the rent. You have recently secured employment but believe you are going to be worse off financially and you want advice on how to deal with your finances.*

(c) *You have been recently bereaved of your spouse of 35 years. When married you spent all your time together, pursued no separate interests and now feel at a loss. The future seems particularly bleak. Although you do not feel that any good will come of it, you visit a local social work agency on the advice of your sister who has used the service herself some time ago.*

(d) *For some time you have been feeling 'out of sorts' but cannot describe exactly what you mean by this. You feel as though your body is lagging behind when you wish to move and feel as if you are becoming stone. These thoughts are occupying more and more of your time and you are becoming afraid of having time to think about them. Although you are quite embarrassed about the situation it seems to you to be becoming unbearable. You are therefore seeking help.*

Whatever your starting point, these exercises aim to value your experience thus far and are designed to help you develop further skills of agency practice.

## C H A P T E R   S U M M A R Y

In this chapter, you have been introduced to some practical requirements and steps that you can take to prepare for practice learning. While you will be assessed prior to undertaking practice learning within an agency, and your programmes will have introduced a process of preparation, there are many things you can do to assist the process and to continue this into practice. Indeed, you are likely to get much more from the experience if you have been actively involved in the process and have shared your preparation openly with your practice teacher. Being prepared and forming an initial working relationship with your practice teacher or assessor will be instrumental in forging a productive partnership for learning. Consideration of this will form the basis of the next chapter concerning supervision on practice learning.

**FURTHER READING**

In preparing for practice the best examples of further reading that you can begin with include your course or programme handbooks. These will give you a sense of what is involved and required in practice learning which will help you plan for the experience. It is also useful to consider and read the requirements and standards, especially the following:

**GSCC** (2002) *Code of Practice for Employees.* London: GSCC. (You can gain access to this online at **www.gscc.org.uk/codes_copies.htm**.)

National Occupational Standards for Social Work, which can be accessed at **www.topssengland.net**.

You may also benefit from refreshing your learning about the process of social work practice and read:

**Parker, J. and Bradley, G.** (2003) *Social Work Practice: Assessment, Planning, Intervention and Review.* Exeter: Learning Matters.

# Chapter 4

## Using supervision to enhance practice learning and practice competence

## Introduction

In this chapter you will be introduced to supervision, consultation and mentoring and some of the purposes for which it is used. The responsibilities and accountabilities of the supervision process will be examined from your perspective as a student, that of the practice teacher and, where appropriate, the day-to-day supervisor. You will be taken through a series of activities and reflective exercises to examine what you might do to prepare for supervision sessions and how to use the time effectively and maximise the benefits gained from supervision. You are encouraged to refer back to Chapter 1 and to use some of the suggestions made there for preparing for supervision.

The importance of supervision for enhancing and improving practice will be emphasised and the skills in accurate and effective recording in supervision stressed. As can be seen from the National Occupational Standards, supervision has much to do with accountability and developing professional competence. We will keep this in mind throughout the discussion. The chapter will also look at the importance of 'looking after yourself' in social work practice learning which can be a challenging and demanding time. Advice on using supportive supervision when things go wrong will be discussed as will some of the power issues that arise from different forms of supervision and sharing your learning journey with the person who will be responsible for a significant part of your assessment.

# What is supervision?

There are probably as many models of supervision and approaches to the process and tasks involved as there are supervisors. The development of student supervision in social work represented a significant step in moving towards practice learning. Indeed, before practice teachers and assessors, the term 'student supervisor' was used to identify the person with responsibility for the 'placement' and learning and assessment process. The importance of the task has not diminished, although the term has fallen out of use. Indeed, in a slightly tongue-in-cheek projection into the future of practice learning, Shardlow (2003, p70) suggests a possible return to 'supervising learning in practice'.

The term supervision, however, now seems to promote a degree of awe among students. It has taken on an almost mystical meaning at times, where supervisors are privy to certain skills and knowledge that can only be understood by initiates or those who are qualified as social workers. This knowledge is bestowed, like the laying on of hands, on unwitting supervisees. This can be the case even more so in the supervision of mature social work students who often feel deskilled at having left practice to study or who have developed a belief that their training is a kind of ritual that they must undergo before being pronounced competent to practice. Of course, for some more experienced students a more cynical approach may have developed. This may be the result of poor supervision experiences in the past, or from a perception of supervision as a 'necessary evil' to endure by students who believe they have the knowledge, skills and competence to practice without recourse to others. For others, it may represent a process by which the experts transfer their greater knowledge and skills to novices waiting like an empty chalice to be filled.

It is important to strip away the mystical trappings attached to the processes and tasks involved in supervision and to stress the fundamental importance of supervision to a social worker's professional and personal development, however experienced he or she may be.

The requirements for social work students to receive adequate and regular supervision were emphasised by social work's previous professional body (CCETSW, 1996). While the amount, regularity or purpose of supervision during practice learning is not specified for the social work degree, it is generally recognised as an integral component of the learning process. Indeed, many programmes have transferred to the degree what they believe is best practice in supervision from their Diploma in Social Work courses. It is, therefore, important to determine what supervision comprises and how it is to be understood.

Hawkins and Shohet (2000) define supervision from a counselling and psychotherapeutic perspective, describing its functions and process. In surveying the literature on supervision, they identify the following core themes running throughout the definitions. Supervision serves to benefit supervisee and service user by developing the practitioner's skills, understanding and ability. Supervision in social work has been identified as comprising three main functions. It is:

- educative and formative;

- supportive or restorative; and

- administrative or normative (see Kadushin, 1976).

These three key elements permeate the literature concerning the nature and purpose of supervision (Ford and Jones, 1987; Brown and Bourne, 1996; Shardlow and Doel, 1996).

# Social work supervision and consultation

Ford and Jones (1987) wrote specifically about the supervision of social work students at a time when supervision formed the core of the practice learning relationship. Their views still hold good for the degree. They present a view of supervision that is a negotiated and contracted arrangement made between student and supervisor, stating:

> *By* supervision, *we mean planned, regular periods of time that the student and supervisor spend together discussing the student's work in the placement and reviewing the learning progress.*
>
> (Ford and Jones, 1987, p63)

They make an important distinction between supervision and consultation, although the two are sometimes used synonymously and you will, during the course of practice learning, engage in both. They acknowledge that consultation may be needed at other times than planned and regular supervision sessions. However, it is a service that can be provided by colleagues or, indeed, other professionals who do not carry the administrative responsibility for carrying through recommended action (Kadushin, 1977). Accountability for this consultation remains with the practice teacher or assessor. The immediate objective of consultation is professional development of the consultee facilitated by the use of a recognised expert.

> *Consultation is regarded as an interactional helping process – a series of sequential steps taken to achieve some objective through an interpersonal relationship. One participant in the transaction has greater expertise, greater knowledge, greater skill in the performance of some particular, specialized function, and this person is designated consultant. The consultee, generally a professional, has encountered a problem in relation to his job which requires the knowledge, skill and expertise of the consultant for its solution or amelioration. Consultation is thus distinguished from other interpersonal interactional processes involving the giving and taking of help, such as casework, counseling, psychotherapy, by virtue of the fact that its problem-solving focus is related to some difficulties encountered in performing job-related functions and by virtue of the fact that the identity of the consultee is generally restricted to someone engaged in implementing professional roles.*
>
> (Kadushin, 1977, pp25–6)

The consultation role is one of problem-solving. It is likely that you will use your day-to-day supervisor and others within the agency as consultants. This may form part of your wider learning that will be reviewed and considered within supervision sessions with your practice teacher or assessor, who is responsible for the overall practice learning experience.

However, Ford and Jones (1987) see the task of the social work supervisor as maximising learning opportunities for the student within the agency context. Thus there is a clear emphasis on the educational role, which accords with the contemporary role of learning in practice. The supervisor acts between the systems involved in practice learning, as both supervisor, with responsibility to agency and service user, and practice teacher, with a responsibility to the educational establishment and student (see Figure 4.1).

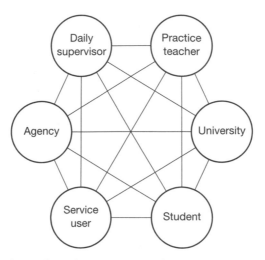

**Figure 4.1** *The interrelationship of systems in student supervision*

It is, of course, the educative function that is emphasised in most definitions (Shulman, 1993; Shardlow and Doel, 1996). This concerns the interpersonal context designed to increase the reflective and critical practice competence of the supervisee (Doel and Shardlow, 1998). The administrative or managerial functions are also important (see Kadushin, 1976). The managerial function acts as a quality-control mechanism that seeks to protect service users, carers and others coming into contact with the agency. The practice teacher-supervisor ensures that work has been completed in accordance with agency procedures and policies. The supervisor often shares responsibility with the supervisee for ensuring that the work is ethical and appropriate. This shared responsibility distinguishes supervision from consultancy which is aimed at providing peer support and advice without shared responsibility (Hawkins and Shohet, 2000). The managerial or administrative function is also concerned with assessment of practice. The tension between supervision and assessment is clear and can cause some concern. However, it is important to acknowledge that tensions exist to prevent them adversely affecting the student–supervisor relationship.

The supportive function of supervision allows the student social worker to explore and deal with the stresses arising from the work itself and the learning process. You should use supervision as a means of gaining support, sharing burdens and expressing some of the emotional challenges of the work. Attention is paid to the supportive side of the process but there has been a tendency to ignore the dangerous potential of the supervisory relationship to become almost a therapy session without a corresponding recognition that emotional support is needed for all practitioners in the helping professions. It is worth remembering that your supervision sessions as a social work student are not therapy but are concerned with the process of learning to practise in a competent manner. The emphasis on practice competence and the necessity to provide clear observable evidence for the assessment of practice may lead some supervisors to neglect further the need for support within a secure supervisory relationship. However, the need is recognised for developing a relationship that is trusted, supportive and provides an outlet or release system when dealing with emotionally taxing work. Supervision is not therapy but a developmental learning process that attends to the needs of the person at an emotional as well as an intellectual, professional and personal level. You will need to know the limits and boundaries for supervision and should seek to clarify these with your practice teacher as soon as possible. Indeed, when negotiating the learning agreement (see Chapter 3), you should clarify supervision practice.

---

ACTIVITY **4.1**

*The following case study provides an example of supervision becoming blurred with therapy. Think of other possible examples where this might happen and suggest some possible ways of avoiding supervision becoming therapy.*

---

CASE STUDY

*Jill was coming to the end of her final practice learning opportunity. She was a successful and hard-working student who had impressed her practice teacher with her confident and competent approach to practice and learning. Jill had been to visit a woman who had had a child adopted before she met her present husband. The woman had recently been approached to make contact with her son who was now aged 21 years. She wanted to meet him but had never told her husband about the adoption.*

*Jill was visibly upset at the next supervision session, and stated to her practice teacher that she too had a child who was adopted and she has not told her partner of ten years about this. The practice teacher discussed how this might impact on her work and explored ways of dealing with the situation in a developmental and supportive way. However, he also offered her six sessions to explore the meaning of this experience for her, thus merging a potentially cathartic relationship with one of practice learning and supervision..*

---

By focusing on a clear supervision agreement that specifies the purpose of the process and the tasks and roles of those involved, you can begin to offset some of the potential dangers of blurring the purpose of sessions. An agreement and outline of roles and expectations are considered later in this chapter. If the work you are involved in does raise concerns you should seek the advice of your practice coordinator and your personal tutor or any advice and support offered by your university.

As Kadushin (1976) notes, the three functions of supervision are complementary. They reflect the goal-oriented nature of the supervisory process and task. Supervision aims to promote and ensure that the most effective and efficient service possible is offered. He offers a definition of the role of the social work supervisor that can also be used to describe the student supervisor:

> ... a social work supervisor is an agency administrative staff member to whom authority is delegated to direct, coordinate, enhance, and evaluate the on-the-job performance of the supervisees for whose work he is held accountable. In implementing this responsibility the supervisor performs administrative, educational, and supportive functions in interaction with the supervisee in the context of a positive relationship. The supervisor's ultimate objective is to deliver to agency clients the best possible service, both quantitatively and qualitatively, in accordance with agency policies and procedures. Supervisors do not directly offer service to the client, but they do indirectly affect the level of service offered through their impact on the direct service supervisees. Supervision is, thus, an indirect service.
>
> (Kadushin, 1976, p21)

---

### ACTIVITY 4.2

*Think of some ways you might use consultation that differ from supervision and make a note of them.*

*You may have suggested something akin to the following:*

*A colleague in the same office who has a special interest in cognitive-behavioural work with children may be contacted for specific advice or consultation on how you might approach a particular case. You might use supervision, however, to explore how you are developing the use of cognitive-behavioural models in your practice and what this contributes to your learning as a social work student.*

*Supervision may involve consideration and review of the health and safety policy of the agency as part of your induction. However, you may consult with an appointed health and safety officer on particular issues relating to its operation.*

---

Gardiner's (1989) review of the literature relating to the supervision of students found that writing about supervision in the United Kingdom was largely influenced by North American social casework supervision. This has remained the case although the context of practice has shifted from psycho-social models. In classical social work literature, Gardiner (1989) found that the traditional approach to supervision was understood as a form of teaching or instruction that employed psycho-dynamic concepts to promote personal growth and development in student social workers. It is from these approaches that a sense of mystery and hidden meanings developed. This approach is still employed in some forms of counselling supervision. Long and Chambers (1996) base their facilitative model on the development of a therapeutic relationship between supervisor and supervisee. The relationship emphasises co-participation, support, valuation, commitment and personal growth. For them, it is a lifelong process based upon an open, honest and genuine relationship.

Rather than define what he means by social work supervision, however, Gardiner (1989) presents an educative, learning model that progresses through debate and interaction with individual students. In social work, most definitions include varying combinations of these core elements.

Brown and Bourne (1996), writing on agency-employee supervision rather than supervision of students, highlight the difficulties in achieving an adequate definition of supervision because of its many different uses. While acknowledging the usefulness of the tripartite schema developed by Kadushin, they do not wish to enter into a terminological debate and offer a succinct definition emphasising the management function as a starting point for discussion.

> *Supervision is the primary means by which an agency-designated supervisor enables staff, individually and collectively, and ensures standards of practice. The aim is to enable the supervisee(s) to carry out their work, as stated in their job specification, as effectively as possible. Regular arranged meetings between supervisor and supervisee(s) form the core of the process by which the supervisory task is carried out. The supervisee is an active participant in this interactional process.*
>
> (Brown and Bourne, 1996, p9)

Their definition includes the main elements of education, quality control and promoting best possible practice. While no doubt the supportive element is included within the context of the interactive relationship between supervisor and supervisee it is implicit rather than explicit. It is referred to more directly in their debate concerning a value base for supervision. They see the process as person-centred and the relationship element and feelings of the supervisee are accorded equal importance alongside managerial and administrative functions.

## Practice learning and supervision

The emphasis in the Diploma in Social Work was upon practice teaching rather than supervision. The fear that this may have promoted a shift in focus from deeper levels of learning and reflection upon the processes involved in that learning (Gardiner, 1989) to instructional models was not realised. The guidance is, however, important. The supervision of students in practice learning situations was considered essential to the collection of evidence, the identification of needs and to enable and facilitate learning to promote and assess competence (CCETSW, 1996). In fact, as mentioned earlier, regular supervision and support is also considered important for the newly qualified worker dealing with complex tasks. This is no less the case for social work students studying for the degree although, as we have mentioned earlier, there are no specific criteria relating to supervision in the requirements for the degree (Department of Health, 2002).

In order to demonstrate the development of professional competence student social workers must acquire and apply a range of knowledge and skills included in the National Occupational Standards, comprising an awareness of how to act and present when working with service users and an ability to reflect upon this. To do so, you must develop skills to analyse your practice in a manner that identifies strengths and learning needs and also become able to transfer this knowledge and skill to other areas of professional practice. It is important, therefore, to be able to show an understanding of the purpose and models of supervision, the use of contracts or agreements in supervision, learning styles and analysis of training and development needs and a commitment to continuing professional development.

Supervision represents a major locus of discussion, teaching and assessment and so contributes to the overall process of the assessment of competence (see Chapter 5). However, very little is specified concerning the actual processes of or tasks that should be involved in supervision and practice teaching. All that is clear is that practice learning should be supervised. It is likely that this will include direct observations of your work with service users. At regular intervals throughout the programme, progress reviews should be completed. These may take place at the mid-point of the assessed practice learning experience or more frequently, and a written assessment of competence made at the end. Supervision and practice teaching were integrated in the former qualification, and the professional body sought to stress the importance of the role:

> CCETSW intends that all students' practice should be supervised by an accredited practice teacher or a practice teacher under assessment for the Practice Teaching Award.
>
> (CCETSW, 1996, p39)

They did recognise the difficulties of reaching this position and added some minimum standards. In the new degree, because of continuing difficulties in retaining qualified practice teachers and in training adequate numbers, the specific emphasis is not made and the focus has shifted to assessment. However, good assessment depends on good supervisory practice, and if you are to know what you must do to pass your practice learning opportunity and have a view as to how you are progressing, you will need regular supervision. Kearney (2003) has presented a four-stage framework indicating who can act as a supervisor/practice assessor, suggesting that at the early stages the person need not be fully qualified as a practice teacher but when it comes to the overall assessment this should be undertaken by a practice teacher with the full award. These are social workers who are likely to provide a constructive, educative supervisory experience.

Most discussions concerning supervision in social work emphasise the educative function and the importance supervision has for encouraging best practice by its quality assurance and accountability function. Alongside these tasks, however, supervision in practice learning is a developmental process that rests upon a clear and supportive relationship between supervisor and supervisee. Similar debates concerning the deployment of effective supervision have taken place in physiotherapy where there has been a similar movement towards an educative model (Cross, 1994) and health visiting where the managerial and supportive functions are evident (Byrne, 1994). Supervision in the nursing context emphasises the skilled professional and developmental approach (Fowler, 1995; Hart and Rotem, 1995; McCormack and Hopkins, 1995; Bishop, 1994). Supervision is defined, to a large extent, by its purpose. This reflects the agency culture and remit. In social work, the emphasis must be upon the roles and responsibilities of the profession as reflected in the National Occupational Standards and subject benchmark statement, as well as the education, support and supervisory management of the individuals involved.

Hogan (2002, p47) emphasises the creative and collaborative aspects of supervision, seeing it as 'an opportunity for the creation of a conversational relationship between two or more parties interested in jointly moving towards shared and more equal ways of relating to each other.' The model suggests starting with an exploration of how the student learns, how feedback should be shared and what each expects of the other. The supervisory process can progress to a solution-oriented approach to learning that identifies what the goals are and what constitutes evidence of having reached them.

There is no one correct way of approaching or undertaking supervision (Thompson et al., 1994). It is important, however, to have an understanding of the models employed, and to recognise the experiences that supervisors bring to the task and process and the different experiences and expectations brought by students. A key element must be: what do you want from supervision? The next section examines some of these issues.

# Models of supervision

In the previous section, supervision was separated into its three main constitutive parts: the educative function, the administrative function and the expressive-emotional-supportive function. Most models consider all three elements to be important although perhaps emphasise different aspects according to purpose and context.

Models of supervision in social work and the helping professions tend to stress the developmental approach and we shall focus on this approach here. The style and approach of both supervisor and supervisee changes as each develops through particular stages of learning. Hawkins and Shohet (2000) synthesise the work of Stoltenberg and Delworth (1987) concerning developmental stages in learning and other models. They describe the four levels of supervisee development as a backdrop to their process model of supervision.

- Level One is characterised by the student's *dependence* upon the supervisor. The student may display a great deal of apprehension at this stage, especially at the prospect of work being assessed. The supervisor's role at this stage is to structure the learning environment, to provide positive feedback and encouragement and to enable the student to focus on what actually happens in practice.

- At Level Two initial anxieties have been overcome. The students are now seen to fluctuate between *dependency and autonomy*, between overconfidence and being overwhelmed. The supervisee becomes more focused but now tests out and challenges the authority and competence of the supervisor. Students may not accept the advice and suggestions of the supervisor, or may believe and express that they are not learning from supervision. They may even directly criticise the supervisor. This can be a turbulent stage.

- By Level Three there is an increased level of *professional self-confidence*. The students can adjust their approach to meet the individual needs of the clients, and can place them in a wider context. The particular theoretical orientation of the students has now been integrated into their personality. It may be no longer transparent nor simply a range of learnt and applied techniques.

- Level Four is the 'master' level characterised by *personal autonomy*, awareness of professional and personal developmental needs, insight and security. This stage is about allowing the knowledge to be deepened and integrated until it becomes practice wisdom.

---

**CASE STUDY**

*Peter's anxieties were evident during the first week of his practice learning and he checked everything he did with his practice teacher, including asking three times when he could go for lunch and checking how to record telephone calls after each one made. During the first month, however, his confidence increased to the point at which he returned to the office late after visiting a service user following lunch without recording this in the office and challenging the supervisor when she asked where he had been. Reasons of health and safety and protection were examined and agreed for the recording of visits. By the latter half of the practice learning opportunity, Peter was able to plan his days and weeks, sharing these with his practice teacher during supervision but confident in the knowledge that he was planning in accordance with the agency procedures.*

Hawkins and Shohet (2000) make the point that such a developmental approach to learning may have analogies with aspects of human growth and development (see also Crawford and Walker, 2003), and the stages of apprenticeship in medieval craft guilds – novice, journeyman, independent craftsman, master craftsman. There may also be links with stages in group development, such as inclusion/exclusion, authority, affection and intimacy. There is a recognition that supervisors are themselves passing through stages. However, they believe it provides a base for their process model of supervision. They suggest that the developmental model is a useful tool in helping supervisors to be more effective in assessing the needs of their supervisees. It also helps in realising that part of the task of supervision is to help in the development of the student as a professional. An interesting facet of their model is that it stresses that as the supervisee develops so must the nature of the supervision.

Although their process model was constructed for counsellors and psychotherapists it can be used equally well in social work practice learning. It focuses on the relationship between supervisor and supervisee rather than the organisational context, but acknowledges that all supervision situations involve four core elements:

- supervisor;
- supervisee;
- service user;
- work context.

The supervisor and supervisee are always present while the service user and work context may be indirectly present by bringing tapes, written reports, role-play and expectations into the supervision session. In your experience of supervision, however, it may be that service users, carers or others are directly involved. Supervision may include observation of direct practice or seeking feedback from others who have seen your work. This reflects both the educative-assessment function of supervision that you will experience and the need for flexible and creative approaches to the process that will, hopefully, maximise your chances for learning (see Hogan, 2002).

The process described by Hawkins and Shohet (2000) involves two interlocking systems, a therapy system and a supervision system. The task of the supervision system is to pay attention to the therapy system. We would not use the term 'therapy', perhaps, in social work supervision but we can supplement the word 'intervention' or 'action' here to make it relevant to our context. The process is separated into how the 'therapy' is reported and reflected upon, and how the 'therapy process' is reflected in the process of supervision. This gives rise to six modes of supervision:

- The therapy or intervention is reported and reflected upon in supervision:

  - reflection on the content of the direct work;

  - exploration of strategies and interventions used by the worker;

  - exploration of the interventive process and relationship.

- Focus on the therapy or intervention as it is reflected in the supervision process. (Some of the terms used are taken from psychodynamic theory, and need further explanation. Transference occurs when students transfer unconscious feelings, attitudes and ideas from practice situations onto the supervisor. Counter-transference occurs when the supervisor reacts in some way to the transference of students. Projection relates to unwanted ideas associated with something the person wishes to protect being projected onto another person or thing.)

  - Focus on the therapist's counter-transference; an exploration of personal material reactivated by the session being described; the transferential role into which the client casts the therapist; consideration of the therapist's unconscious attempt at counter-transference; projected material from service users that the therapist has taken in either physically or mentally.

  - Focus on the relationship in supervision as a mirror of the session.

  - Focus on the supervisor's counter-transference and the thoughts and feelings aroused by discussion of therapy; the responses used to provide reflective illumination for the therapist.

Hawkins and Shohet (2000) suggest that all modes of supervision are employed in a good supervisory relationship but not all in the same session. The various modes depend upon the developmental stage of the supervisee. This is a model that is used in psychotherapy and counselling but you may find yourself involved in such a supervisory process depending on the agency in which you are undertaking practice learning and on the theoretical orientation of your practice teacher. It is likely that your supervision will involve close scrutiny of your cases and you should prepare by compiling a list of cases you are working with, visits you have undertaken and what went on during these visits. You may not need to examine the process using the psychodynamic concepts introduced above, but you will be required to reflect deeply on what occurred, what explanations there may be, what alternative ways of working there might be and what key aspects of learning now need to be assimilated.

As a way of beginning to reflect more deeply on your work, consider some of the ways in which psychodynamic concepts may be used in supervision during your practice learning as an educative, supportive and/or administrative tool.

It is likely that these concepts relate mainly to educative-reflective and supportive roles rather than administrative and managerial aspects of supervision. The following case study provides an example of how the concepts may figure within the supervisory process.

### CASE STUDY

Amrita had been feeling unsupported in her practice learning since a supervision session two weeks previously. Amrita explained this to her practice teacher. They looked back at the previous session in which Amrita described some of the difficulties she was having engaging with a service user who was experiencing domestic violence but did not wish to leave her partner. Amrita believed that her practice teacher was being unhelpful and preventing her from working with this woman constructively. She transferred her frustration with the case to her practice teacher, who reacted against this by withdrawing from offering advice, triggering memories of advice she had been given some years ago which led to an unhappy and difficult outcome in a similar case. When the practice teacher and Amrita were able to explore this it provided an opportunity to move forward, acknowledging that the perceptions and frustrations were not personal.

Gardiner (1989) also proposes using a developmental model. He does so with social work students in mind. He stresses that there is a developmental continuum comprising three levels of interaction:

- surface-reproductive conceptualisation – facts and procedures are recounted, and the relationship between student and supervisor is hierarchical;

- active-constructive search for meaning, which is a more horizontal process that uses negotiation and debate;

- focus on learning to learn – reflection on the process (meta-learning) (see Chapter 2).

The three levels of learning are observed in supervision as student social workers develop in their practice learning. In the first stage, the focus is upon content and learning is predominantly passive. It is dependent upon the belief that one can learn the right way to practise. When students reach the second stage they recognise diversity in practice and become actively involved in the learning process sharing with the practice teacher and negotiating meanings. At the third stage, students recognise and demonstrate versatility in their approaches to learning and become able to transfer both content and process to other settings.

Brown and Bourne (1996) recognise the importance of developmental approaches to their systemic model of supervision. The model includes four systems that interact with one another:

- practice system;

- worker system;

- team system;

- agency system.

The model is said to operate at three levels of complexity representing a distinct developmental stage. The induction phase provides a clear operational understanding of the various systems. This is akin to the factual reproduction stage or focus on content. Following this, a more sophisticated level of exploration occurs in the connection phase. At this stage the connections between systems are considered. This includes:

- the professional – practice-worker systems interface;

- the collaborative – worker-team systems interface;

- the managerial – team-agency systems interface;

- the organisational – agency-practice systems interface.

Finally, within supervision, in the integration phase, there is a synthesis of all four systems.

Brown and Bourne (1996) write for professionals in qualified practice and not for students. Their model is important, however, in demonstrating the fluidity and complex nature of social work as opposed to the more focused activity of counselling or psychotherapy, and, in this regard, it is a useful adjunct to the process model (Hawkins and Shohet, 2000).

---

**CASE STUDY**

*If we consider Peter's development throughout his practice learning we can see that at the induction stage he was embedded within the practice system, relying on his practice teacher for guidance and approval at every turn. As he progressed to fix his own appointments and to manage his week, we saw him connect more to the team and agency systems and to begin to collaborate with others in the team. Towards the end of his practice learning experience Peter was able to use supervision to share responsibility and maintain accountability for his practice, as well as identify learning needs and evidence that would be used within his final assessment.*

---

Shardlow and Doel (1996) write about changes in practice teaching which emphasised the educative responsibility of the practice teacher. They employ the term teaching role and emphasise this active task of practice teachers as distinct from the earlier supervisory role which, in their view, was passive. It is this understanding that underpins their practice tutorial model.

In this model, the practice teacher acts as coordinator of the student's learning in practice. Using a structured approach to learning assists the practice teacher and student to determine future learning needs, methods of learning and the assessment of competence. In acknowledging differences in the way people learn it shares many elements with the developmental approaches outlined above. The context for learning is given as the practice tutorial which is described in the following way.

> A 'practice tutorial' is a meeting between student and practice teacher to enable the student's practice learning. It is formal to the extent that it is pre-planned, with an agenda. It commonly takes place at weekly intervals. Using the terminology practice tutorial firmly locates this event within the orbit of teaching, by using language conventionally associated with learning rather than with the managerial connotations of supervision.

(Shardlow and Doel, 1996, p. 106)

In qualified social work practice, supervision may include an element of learning but its primary focus is, according to Shardlow and Doel (1996), to ensure managerial accountability for the social work practitioner's work. However, they do acknowledge the managerial and administrative function of the practice tutorial. The emphasis upon teaching is important and recognises the central role of social workers in promoting your development in practice learning. However, the change of name may be challenged. The practice tutorial seems to indicate use of an instructional approach that may separate practice learning from its professional context. Student social workers are educated for agency practice. In all models of supervision there appears to be emphasis laid upon the developmental and educative functions (Shulman, 1993). To minimise the function of managerial accountability for practice, however, may detract from learning for professional and accountable practice. Since practice learning often takes place within the context of legally defined social work services there is a need to maintain this level of accountability. It is inconceivable that any agency would exclude such accountability from its student practitioners. Good practice is accountable and the student's learning and development is characterised by integrating the many complex levels of practice within professional social work. There are also issues of power that need to be addressed by a negotiated, developmental learning approach.

The supervision session is contextual in any agency. The supportive and managerial functions are located at the interface of the three following interlocking systems:

- the interactional (the student, other professional and service users);

- the personal (student–supervisor relationship);

- power relations (student and supervisor).

These, in turn, are influenced by the wider system of practice learning, such as the university's expectations, individual student learning needs and requirements, expectations and standards set for social work education. The following case study provides an example of where student supervision sits in relation to agency practice:

*Jane was about halfway through her first practice learning opportunity. She wanted to talk about a particular case with which she was working. She had seen the family the previous evening who had disclosed to her their negative feelings towards the eldest child, Tom, aged 13. She said that they had implied he was nothing but trouble, kept running away rather than face up to his responsibilities, had sworn at his mother and hit his younger brother and sister on numerous occasions. Jane said she was particularly worried about the father's statement that he would 'put Tom in hospital if he carried on'.*

*The practice teacher was also concerned by this situation. Recognising Jane's need to voice her distress at the statements and concern for the young person formed part of the session. The practice teacher believed, however, that Jane still had more to say. By asking her to relate the process of the session and what she thought should now be done it transpired that the mother had recently thrown two snooker balls at Tom, meaning to hit him, but had missed, and that physical punishments represented the family's usual approach to discipline.*

*While there was a legitimate concern for the student's well-being and a necessity to view this situation and her response to it as part of her education there was also a need to take action to ensure that the young person involved was protected. This led to a constructive and frank discussion concerning child protection issues, confidentiality and the rights of families. It also led to facing the more difficult issues of practice within a safe and supported environment.*

Student supervision sessions are developmental and about learning but also concern the tasks and functions of managing work with service users in a safe and ethical way. It is essential that service users are given the highest quality of service possible and supervision is one tool designed to help ensure this is the case. The session provides a clear, focused forum for exploring the casework undertaken. It also provides a forum for student support. Let us return to the case study of Jane for a moment:

*As mentioned above, Jane was in her first assessed practice placement. She was 21 years old and had 12 months' voluntary experience in a hostel for homeless people. She demonstrated a clear capacity for recognising ethical tensions and difficult decisions. She also showed a remarkable aptitude for gaining knowledge. However, she did display a tendency to see good and potential in everyone. This caused her some difficulties when determining who was her client and also caused problems when working with the policy and procedures of the agency. Supervision, therefore, was focused towards learning the workings of the agency, determining who the primary client may be and establishing priorities and reasons for this in terms of legislation, policy, procedure and ethics. The incident mentioned above was a constructive pivotal point in her practice learning from which Jane learned a great deal and managed to develop skills of liaison with other professionals, and to use supervision to gain the support and advice she needed.*

The process of supervision should contain both formal learning and a developmental element. There are many different roles and functions of supervision in practice learning that allow student social workers to develop and progress through the various levels of learning described by Gardiner (1989). This can be achieved within an agency context in which practitioners are accountable for their work but their level of experience, learning needs and expectations are taken into account. It is important that student social workers are provided with a supportive and flexible learning environment in which practice is discussed, reflected upon and monitored.

Support, negotiation and a concern for shared learning does not mean that authority cannot be used constructively to assist your learning. Indeed, there is supportive evidence to indicate that use of authority in social work supervision can be appreciated. Munson (1981) found that supervisor–supervisee interaction and satisfaction with the process was significantly greater when the supervisor's authority was seen to derive from competence. This can be achieved where student social workers are aided by competent research-minded practitioners to experience and develop the knowledge, skills and values integral to contemporary social work practice. To achieve this, student social workers and practice teachers/supervisors operate together in collaboration according to skills, needs and developmental stage (Kadushin, 1977) through a process of both consultation and supervision. The emphasis is on learning and the educative function is designed to improve professional impact and practice and to aid work in the organisational setting (Shulman, 1993). Supervision is not distinct from social work practice (Brashears, 1995). In fact, it is seen as an integral part of practice not only important to morale but to continuing professional development (Rautkis and Koeske, 1994). We will now consider a model which in many ways is a synthesis of the developmental and structured approaches discussed above that suggests ways of preparing for and using supervision to enhance your practice learning.

# An agency model of supervision

## The supervision agreement or contract

An important aspect of good supervision is to negotiate a clear agreement at the outset of the practice learning opportunity. This agreement needs to be clear, explicit and focused. While there are many aspects of the agreement that will be agency or university led, you should be able to be involved in the negotiation of specific aspects of the agreement as this will, to some extent, structure your learning and your relationship with your practice teacher as supervisor. A model of such a contract can be seen in Figure 4.2. This is set on two levels and as such may be described on both vertical and horizontal axes. No doubt your university and the agencies in which you undertake your practice learning will have their own supervision agreements. This model, however, may help you structure and understand some of the processes involved.

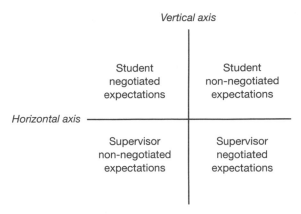

*Figure 4.2* *Level of supervision contract*

The vertical axis of the agreement acknowledges the organisational and managerial functions of supervision. The supervisor/practice teacher and agency need to control and assure the quality of practice. This level sets down the specific expectations and non-negotiable criteria for supervision. The unequal power relations can be made explicit here. It may be argued that making such inequalities explicit only serves the interests of those setting the terms of your learning as a social worker and precludes collaborative effort aimed at developing practice. However, the context of the arrangements are made clear, as are the purposes of supervision. Indeed, because you are being educated for a professional and academic qualification there are bound to be set criteria for learning. This model, however, allows collaboration over individual and flexible aspects and is, therefore, more open.

Social work education is not solely a linear and progressive process of learning and development, of course. Although the horizontal axis of the supervisory agreement may suggest progression along a continuum it is important to acknowledge the dynamic interactive elements of supervision and the necessity of beginning with the student's experience, skills, knowledge and building on his or her strengths. Particular elements and needs can be negotiated and included to make the agreement individual and specific. An element of partnership is introduced. The following copy of a supervision contract exemplifies these distinct levels.

### SUPERVISION CONTRACT
#### between
#### A. Supervisor and Chris Stevens

#### Aim
*This agreement aims to detail arrangements for formal supervision sessions, to delineate practical matters, and specify reciprocal tasks, expectations and renegotiation arrangements.*

## Basis

*This agreement has been discussed and negotiated between the two partici-
pants mentioned above. It will cover the period of Chris's first practice learning
opportunity at the Greentrees Team. The dates of the practice learning opportunity are as follows: 4 January 2005 – 23 June 2005.*

## Practical arrangements

1. *Formal supervision sessions will be offered on a weekly basis and will last
   approximately one and a half hours.*

2. *Formal supervision will usually be conducted on an individual basis but, at
   times, group supervision sessions will be held. Sessions will be arranged
   according to the particular needs of Chris and the specific topics and issues
   under discussion.*

3. *Notwithstanding the formal sessions arranged, Chris will be able to contact
   other members of staff for advice, support and case discussion, and will be
   able to avail himself of opportunities for informal day-to-day supervision
   within the Unit.*

4. *Unless otherwise arranged, supervision will take place in A. Supervisor's
   office.*

5. *The timing for each session is as follows: 9.00 am – 10.30 am each Monday
   morning. (It may be necessary to rearrange some of these times. Notice will
   be given in advance if this is the case.)*

## Content of sessions

6. *Each session will discuss, review and critically analyse social work practice.
   Not only will the focus of the session be upon Chris's practice, attention will also
   be given to the identification of learning needs and opportunities and resources
   to meet these, training needs and professional development. There will be
   opportunities within the sessions to discuss more general matters relating to
   professional and personal development as a social work practitioner.*

*Wherever possible, we will discuss ways in which Chris is meeting or can meet
the National Occupational Standards and how he uses theory in practice and
how to record evidence gathered.*

## Expectations

7. *It is expected that both participants to the agreement will be punctual and
   treat the supervision arrangements as a priority.*

8. *If, for any reason, it is not possible to attend, or one of the participants will
   be delayed, it is incumbent upon that individual to contact the other as soon
   as possible and to renegotiate a date and time.*

9. *It is expected that Chris will bring a* written *agenda of issues and topics he wishes to discuss within supervision to at least* ten *sessions. These will help provide evidence illustrating the achievement or otherwise of key roles and units of the National Occupational Standards.*

10. *Specific topics will be discussed at supervision. The context of supervision is set out within the learning agreement. Focus is maintained by adherence to the practice curriculum. Although it is a requirement to demonstrate anti-oppressive and anti-discriminatory practice throughout the practice learning opportunity, at least one session will focus upon the identification, assessment and challenge of oppressive practice in social work.*

11. *It is expected that aspects of the* law *relating to social work in this agency, to* special *issues and* service *users worked with, and particular models for practice will form part of supervisions sessions. Chris may be required to bring material he has researched for presentation at these sessions.*

12. *Chris can expect* honesty *from the practice teacher and other staff in the Unit. Where aspects of his practice are recognised as particular strengths these will be acknowledged and further skills development encouraged. If aspects of Chris's practice cause concern these will be identified and discussed with him at the earliest opportunity within a framework that seeks to identify that which needs to be done to ensure his practice is competent.*

13. *If Chris has any difficulties or issues he wishes to raise he can expect the practice teacher to respond as soon as is practicable. Chris can also approach other members of Greentreees staff.*

## Renegotiation and review

14. *This agreement can be changed after discussion with both parties and to mutual satisfaction.*

15. *If at any time the agreement does not seem to be working as arranged either party can ask for a complete and comprehensive renegotiation in order to determine a mutually convenient set of arrangements.*

16. *The agreement will be reviewed at three points during the practice learning opportunity. A formal interim review will take place at the midpoint of the practice learning. The date for the midpoint review is 5 April 2005.*

## Specific details

(a) *Case work will be undertaken jointly with the practice teacher.*

(b) *Chris will complete a learning journal to reflect on his experiences throughout the week. This will be used to focus supervision sessions.*

*Signed* .....................................

*Date* .....................................

*A. Supervisor*

*Signed* .....................................

*Date* .....................................

*Chris Stevens*

## Practical arrangements

Formal sessions are, as seen from the agreement above, held weekly and last about one and a half hours. While they are usually individual it is sometimes useful to hold group sessions. Every agency and practice teacher will have his or her own ways of working. Wherever possible, however, you should consider your own learning needs and ensure that your views and preferences are known. Group sessions may take place when complementing a practice curriculum or particular aspects of learning. For instance, discussing anti-oppressive practice may be more productive in group situations. It may be that the group offers a degree of protection to students when identifying possible oppressive practice and discrimination, or it may be helpful as an update to other staff in the agency to join in. However, it is important that group sessions do not hamper the identification and challenge of personal assumptions and values. The following case study provides an example of when a group session was employed to assist the educative and supportive functions of supervision.

CASE STUDY

*Three students were working predominantly in the area of childcare. In many cases they were working collaboratively. While it was important to ensure that agency policy was being adhered to it was also important to use part of the session to review the methods and approaches employed. This represented an important concern for the service user and best possible practice. However, as part of the learning process and to foster peer support each student was allotted the task of finding out and bringing to the next session all that they knew about the social, psychological and physical development of children aged 0–5 years; children aged 6–11 years, and adolescents. Feedback from the students collected informally throughout and formally at the end of the practice learning opportunity indicated their appreciation of this session. It was also interesting to note that these three students performed well in the childcare module taken immediately after practice learning. Their learning was retained and transferred to another setting.*

When in supervision it is important to ensure that you and your practice teacher are committed to the session. Punctuality is important and the value of the session to personal and professional development is emphasised at the outset of the practice learning opportunity. This is also important to the assessment of development of professional competence. The commitment is, however, two-way, and practice teachers must ensure that they prioritise this session. This demonstrates their commitment to you as a learner, as an individual and as a person. The relationship between yourself and the practice teacher represents an invaluable part of the learning process and a demonstration of interestedness and concern from both parties assists the development of rapport.

Bringing an agenda is an important way of preparing for and structuring the session, and it can assist in the achievement of units within the National Occupational Standards and your own portfolio of evidence. If you prepare in this way, you are making it clear to your practice teacher that you are interested in the process and able to make an active contribution. It also allows you to direct some of the focus to matters that are important to you. A prepared agenda may be quite simple, as the example in Figure 4.3 shows:

---

Agenda for Supervision Session

**Student:**      Carol Short

**Practice teacher:**      A. Supervisor

**Date:**      20 February 2005

**Cases for discussion:**      IB, JW, GG, IM

**Issues arising:**      Planning and monitoring task-centred work with IM

     Culture and gender issues

     Interim care orders, JW

**Learning needs and evidence for self-assessment:**

---

*Figure 4.3*   *Example of a supervision agenda*

The venue itself can be an important feature of the session. Supervision must be held in reasonably comfortable surroundings, usually in the individual staff member's offices or in an interview room where offices are open-plan or shared. The venue may change depending on the nature and purpose of the session and is affected by the physical space available to the agency. It is important that sessions are uninterrupted and all staff seek to ensure that supervision sessions are given priority over other responsibilities. This demands that telephones are diverted and that door signs are clearly displayed requesting no interruptions. You have a responsibility as a student social worker for this as much as your practice teacher. One way of ensuring that everyone is aware that you will be unavailable is to complete a weekly planner that can be given to all administrative staff indicating your whereabouts and movements during the week. If this highlights supervision sessions they can be noted by other staff members.

In order to gain as much as you can from supervision you should ensure that all sessions are recorded in written form. This may be either recorded jointly to agree content and plans made, or undertaken by yourself as a learning task. Every agency is different and if supervision sessions are not recorded as a matter of course, you should endeavour to do so as this will help you mark your progress and identify future learning needs. Supervision notes could form part of the portfolio of evidence used when assessing the development of your professional practice throughout the practice learning experience. They form a valuable component of the learning process, aid clarity and ensure a transparency in thinking that helps to offset the power imbalance. An example of written supervision notes is shown in Figure 4.4.

---

**Supervision Notes**

**Student:**                                Carol Short

**Practice Teacher:**                        A Supervisor

**Date:**                                    20 February 2005

**Cases for discussion:**                    IB, JW, GG, IM

Four cases were discussed.

IB, a ten-year-old with behavioural problems, has been away with his parents and, therefore, no visit was made last week. AS suggested reading Sutton's work on troubled children before the next visit.

JW is an eight-year-old girl currently the subject of an interim care order with a full hearing planned for next month. The intention is to return her to her parents in a planned way. Discussion concerning the use of care orders, delays in reaching full hearings and the impact on children and families. AS suggested reading and asked CS to make contact with legal section to learn about their work.

IM is a parent who is finding it difficult to integrate into the local community. CS is working in a task-centred way to assist IM in identifying and joining a local mother's group. CS asked for advice on setting tasks as IM wants 'to have lots of friends and fit in'. CS thinks this is too much and wants advice on agreeing smaller goals while not being directive. Discussion about small achievements, starting from where the client is and planning for success with them while being realistic. Reading given.

**Learning needs and evidence for self-assessment:**

CS identified using theory in practice. This is a need to be developed for the next session. The use of the law and relationship between social work and the legal system will be presented at the next session. CS will report on meeting with legal section.

Discussion of cultural issues held until future session.

---

**Figure 4.4** *Example of supervision notes*

## The tasks and process of supervision

There are a number of core elements to determining the tasks and processes of supervision within any agency context. It is important that supervision is flexible and tailored to meet your individual needs.

**Supervision Matrix**

| | | Supervisory function | | | | |
|---|---|---|---|---|---|---|
| | Task and process | Collaborative | Consultative | Educative | Supportive | Administrative |
| *Developmental stage* | | | | | | |
| Induction | Relationship building; boundary setting; procedure and policy explanation procedure and policy | | | | | |
| Dependency/autonomy | Interview plans; case notes/records; assessments; role play; case studies | | | | | |
| Professional self-confidence | Process recording; reflective and critical analysis of practice; case studies; presentations | | | | | |
| Expertise/skilled wisdom | Teaching; supervision/consultation with others | | | | | |
| *Practice curriculum stage* | | | | | | |
| Introduction | Planning; demonstration; agency working | | | | | |
| Application | Engaging with others; use of methods and skills | | | | | |
| Integration and critical reflection | Transferable learning | | | | | |

**Figure 4.5** *Supervision matrix*

The supervision matrix is a helpful crystallisation of the principles and elements of supervision models (see Figure 4.5). It is flexible and allows you to place yourself at the developmental stage you have reached at a particular point in the practice learning opportunity and to identify with your practice teacher what is needed and what is available within the agency to meet those needs. It is a dynamic tool that will change and develop. It is not meant to be used rigidly but as a guide to assist the professional developmental process through supervision.

The following case study example of supervision will help to illustrate the model.

---

**CASE STUDY**

*Chris Stevens came into social work with ten years' experience as a pipe fitter. He had lost his job two years ago and had been engaged since as a volunteer with an agency in his home town working with substance use, while undertaking an Access to Higher Education course at his local college. Chris had left school at 15 with no qualifications and was finding the transition from college to degree education a difficult one to make. He was offered a practice learning opportunity with a specialist multi-agency unit after expressing an interest in working with people with autism. At the initial placement meeting Chris expressed some bitterness and regret that his previous job had finished and had some reservations about his skills and potential to work as a social worker.*

*After discussion with Chris, the practice teacher concluded that he was at the beginning stages of development, had considerable anxiety about the prospect of social work practice and would need strong support to develop his confidence and reach his potential. The practice teacher negotiated the contract shown above with Chris. They then decided together that Chris would compile a pen picture of his life experience including a description of some of the reasons that led him into social work education. This would form the basis of discussion at the first agreed supervision session. In addition, Chris would bring a list of his strengths and needs as he understood them.*

*At the first session, Chris brought with him a brief description of his work as a pipe fitter. It concentrated largely upon his feelings of ill-treatment at the hands of his previous employers. Chris had not managed to compile a list of strengths and needs. He stated that he was not entirely sure what was expected of him and the practice teacher was alerted again to his high levels of anxiety. In order to introduce Chris into the agency in a gentle and supported manner the practice teacher negotiated an induction that involved a guided search of agency policy, procedure and staffing. Chris was set a number of tasks comprising collecting information relating to the organisation and to work undertaken with service users. Consideration of his strengths and needs was put back until the next session.*

*It was through these mutually negotiated tasks that the process of building rapport was gradually achieved. Chris was given support to complete the tasks and was provided with learning goals and objectives designed to increase his knowledge and skills. He was provided with case material to read and comment upon in discussion with his practice teacher. He was provided with a range of contact names and numbers in a variety of agencies to approach and find out about roles and responsibilities, and how access could*

---

*be gained to these agencies. This he compiled into a 'resource directory' for use by himself and others in the agency. This process took account of the responsibility of the agency to its service users and it was not until a degree of confidence and competence had been established and assessed that Chris was allowed to take on casework.*

*One part of each supervision session that Chris expressed a degree of satisfaction with was the review of the previous session. He said that this made him feel as though he had been listened to and that his needs were treated as important. He also said that it ensured that tasks were completed because he knew they would be checked.*

*As the practice learning opportunity proceeded, Chris became less dependent upon the practice teacher to explain every detail of agency procedure and to accompany him on each casework visit. However, it was noted that Chris was not bringing procedural matters to supervision sessions at all. When questioned about this he seemed affronted and told the practice teacher that he thought he had gone past this stage and had proved that he knew the procedures and policies and felt able to 'do some real work'. Instead of confronting Chris about this the practice teacher suggested that they devote some of the time of the session to discussing interview plans and assessments made. Following this, they agreed to video record a role play of an interview between practitioner and client. The video recording was then discussed. Chris was perceptive enough to see that his approach to the service user was based upon a number of assumptions he had made about the statements made to him. However, when challenged, he argued strongly in favour of his approach because, in his words, it was derived from 'common sense'.*

*At this point, the practice teacher believed Chris had reached a critical stage in development. He had, in fact, become stuck in his own assumptions, finding it difficult to accept the advice and experience of the practice teacher and agency. While this can be a valuable stage, it was worrying in Chris's case because he was not prepared to see any other point of view. The practice teacher decided to take a number of steps back. The value base and principles of the agency were reconsidered. Following this, it was suggested to Chris that they undertake the role play again but change roles. This was again video recorded. The practice teacher took the role of the service user but changed the way the service user was responded to by reflecting the content of Chris's statements and the feelings he expressed, allowing him to talk freely but summarising the main issues arising without making quick judgements concerning the main issues and concerns. Chris was asked to comment on the approach and to highlight differences in his own approach. This illuminated the value of alternative approaches and demonstrated to him continuing learning needs which, within the supervision session, they could plan to meet.*

*Role play proved a useful resource that helped to develop Chris's reflective and critical skills. Process recordings of casework were made to take this development further and Chris's rising confidence in his own ability to complete tasks was tempered by a measured approach that identified alternatives and the underlying values that Chris brought to his practice.*

*The educational function of supervision remained high throughout the practice learning. The concerns raised by Chris's inexperience and rigid approach to practice meant that the*

> *managerial and quality assurance functions remained high in profile also. However, given Chris's special needs in coming to terms with his dismissal from his previous job and moving into a new area of work a supportive role was also necessary throughout. It was the combination of all three functions that provided Chris with the opportunities to develop as a social worker.*

Supervision is not an easy experience and you should be prepared, as was Chris, for some plain speaking from your practice teacher and other supervisors. Remember, there are many functions to supervision but learning to practise, as a student, is central. When you are learning you will receive advice, guidance and direction. At times, it may be necessary for you to step back in the process or to retread what seems to be older ground. This is important to your professional development and accepting this as part of supervised practice will help you gain most from the practice learning experience.

## C H A P T E R   S U M M A R Y

In this chapter we have reviewed some of the ways in which the term supervision is employed in social work and the helping professions. The main models of supervision have been outlined and an approach distilled and synthesised from these models has been presented and exemplified using case material from practice learning opportunities. It has been important in this chapter to spend some time introducing these models so you can prepare for the range of uses of supervision that you may come into contact with. The tripartite approach to supervision – educative, administrative and supportive – and the developmental stage model have been integrated to provide an approach that respects the educational function of practice learning within the 'real-life' context of social work. The managerial role and necessity of promoting accountable practice have been acknowledged and discussed.

Preparation for supervision will help the process and you have a considerable role to play here in preparing agendas, ensuring that your notes and written material are available and completing case résumés for discussion. Supervision sessions are valuable in checking and maintaining your progress in the agency. Your supervisor will begin the process of assessment within these sessions and the more prepared you are and the more able you are to discuss your learning needs in an open and honest way the better. In the next chapter, we will consider the assessment processes involved in practice learning.

**FURTHER READING**

**Doel, M. and Shardlow, S.** (1998) The New Social Work Practice: Exercises and Activities for Training and Developing Social Workers. Aldershot: Arena.
The book provides a range of activities and exercises that will assist you in preparing for and using supervision in an effective way that enhances your learning. The activities are clear and relate to a developmental process of learning covering a broad area.

**Hawkins, P. and Shohet, R.** (2000) Supervision in the Helping Professions: An Individual, Group and Organizational Approach. Buckingham: Open University Press.
This book is a must for those of you with a specific interest in supervision as a subject area in its own right. It is detailed, well researched and provides a comprehensive look at models and uses of supervision.

# *Chapter 5*

## Assessment of practice learning, gathering evidence and demonstrating competence

**ACHIEVING A SOCIAL WORK DEGREE**

This chapter will help you to meet the following National Occupational Standards:
*Key Role 5: Manage and be accountable, with supervision and support, for your own social work practice within your organisation*
- Manage and be accountable for your own work
- Contribute to the management of resources and services
- Manage, present and share records and reports
- Work within multi-disciplinary and multi-organisational teams, networks and systems

*Key Role 6: Demonstrate professional competence in social work practice*
- Research, analyse, evaluate and use current knowledge of best social work practice
- Work within agreed standards of social work practice and ensure own professional development
- Manage complex ethical issues, dilemmas and conflicts
- Contribute to the promotion of best social work practice

It will also introduce you to the range of academic standards as set out in the social work subject benchmark statement, including working ethically in and understanding, theoretically and in practice, social work services, and working with service users in a skilled way.

## Introduction

Practice learning opportunities are rigorously assessed. This demands that students know what is to be assessed and how it will be evaluated. It also requires students to become effective self-assessors, reflecting on learning, identifying needs and working out learning plans to meet those needs within the context of practice. This chapter will examine the assessment process and the requirements and National Occupational Standards to be achieved. We will consider what constitutes evidence and how it can be gathered, displayed and used to demonstrate growing competence. You are encouraged to refer back to the assessment of ethical and anti-oppressive practice as presented in Chapter 1.

The assessment of practice learning and competence in practice is a key element of the practice learning experience. This can create confusion and disquiet for student social workers not least because your daily supervisors and practice teachers or practice learning assessors have a dual responsibility for making an assessment and, ultimately, in making a pass or fail recommendation to your university, as well as teaching and supporting you in your learning. However, the system for assessment is more complex still. All those involved in your practice learning experience may be called upon to provide evidence of your competence to practise (see Figure 5.1).

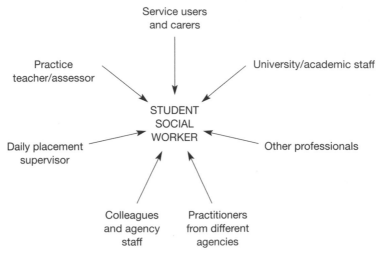

**Figure 5.1** *The range of assessment in practice learning*

It is important to note two things. Firstly, the views and opinions of people you work with is crucial evidence in identifying your learning needs and assessing competence. Secondly, you are, as a student, central to the assessment process, and self-assessment, critique and reflection are skills that add to the process and can be continued into qualified, registered practice.

# Assessment process

## What is assessed and how will it be evaluated?

An enduring and key issue in the assessment of student learning is that students will, if the learning is purely focused on the assessment outcome, do only that which is required to pass or succeed. This may, of course, reduce the level of learning and skills development that can be gained from the experience. This issue is important to bear in mind during your practice learning opportunities. It is inevitable that tutors within your university, your practice teachers and assessors, future employers and yourself will concentrate on achieving a positive outcome: passing the practice experience. Practice learning opportunities for a qualifying degree in social work are likely to focus on the National Occupational Standards for Social Workers, the academic subject benchmarking criteria and the Code of Practice and values for social work. It is these aspects that will we consider below.

Practice learning is central, however, to your development as a beginning practitioner and beyond, once qualified. It is fundamental, therefore, that you engage fully with the experience, gaining in knowledge, skills and values about your practice as a social worker, and, indeed, about yourself as an individual. It is important, therefore, to see the assessment of practice learning not only as an outcome – whether or not you have passed or failed – but also as a process of development. Understanding the assessment of practice in this way can help you construct a focus on the reasons for practice learning and its assessment as a means of developing your professional skills and competence.

You can usefully adapt some of your assessment skills learned in the classroom and in direct practice to assist you in understanding and approaching your own assessment. While a social work assessment is different to judging your development and competence as a social worker, there are some similarities. Parker and Bradley (2003) describe two basic types of assessment:

- ongoing and fluid;

- time-limited and issues-specific.

The process model where assessment is ongoing and fluid considers developmental issues and changes taking into account mediating experiences and, in respect of practice learning, suggests that the experience can be one of continued self-assessed learning as well as being assessed by an experienced and qualified social worker. The description of assessment as time-limited and issues-specific relates to the final, summative assessment of your competence. In practice learning, a focus on both types of assessment will help you gain most from the experience.

Practice learning is assessed as part of many professional programmes but the student perspective has been little considered. Knight (2003) reports on a qualitative study of final-year undergraduate students from an occupational therapy background, investigating their experiences of being assessed. In general, she found that there were high levels of acceptance with the primary assessment but some concern about its reliability. You should study the assessment criteria set for your practice learning experience and level and seek to understand ways in which the criteria might be met. In this way, you will be able to identify the types and sources of evidence to ensure that the assessment tests what it purports to examine. A major influence on the process of the assessment is the 'fieldwork educator' or practice teacher, the supervisory relationship and the learning environment. For your own practice learning, these variables will also be important and your involvement in the matching process, the development of a constructive supervisory relationship and engagement with the practice learning experience are central.

Your involvement in the assessment process is also crucial and we will focus on that in a later section in this chapter. However, when considering assessment, you will probably bring to mind the final assessment of your competence, whether you have passed your practice learning opportunity. This is understandable and it is helpful to keep this in mind throughout, although it is equally important not to become preoccupied with 'passing the practice' at the expense of learning for practice. While it is your learning – and the application of that learning – for competent practice that is assessed, there are set criteria for social work education that will form the basis of that assessment. We will revisit these here.

**NATIONAL OCCUPATIONAL STANDARDS**

Key Role 1: Prepare for and work with individuals, families, carers, groups and communities to assess their needs and circumstances

Key Role 2: Plan, carry out, review and evaluate social work practice, with individuals, families, carers, groups and communities and other professionals

Key Role 3: Support individuals to represent their needs, views and circumstances

Key Role 4: Manage risk to individuals, families, carers, groups, communities, self and colleagues

Key Role 5: Manage and be accountable, with supervision and support, for your own social work practice within your organisation

Key Role 6: Demonstrate professional competence in social work practice

**SUBJECT BENCHMARK CRITERIA FOR SOCIAL WORK**

Social work services and service users
The service delivery context
Values and ethics
Social work theory
The nature of social work practice
- Communication and information technology
- Problem-solving skills
- Communication skills
- Skills in working with others
- Skills in personal and professional development

ASSESSING PRACTICE LEARNING

**GSCC CODE OF PRACTICE**

1. Protect the rights and promote the interests of service users and carers
2. Strive to establish and maintain the trust and confidence of service users and carers
3. Promote the independence of service users while protecting them as far as possible from danger or harm
4. Respect the rights of service users while seeking to ensure that their behaviour does not harm themselves or other people
5. Uphold public trust and confidence in social care services
6. Be accountable for their practice and take responsibility for maintaining and improving their knowledge and skills

*Figure 5.2* *Assessment in practice learning*

There are many underpinning documents for social work education in England, while other countries in the UK may have a more integrated approach. The requirements for social work education and practice detailed by the Department of Health (2002) are vague when it comes to practice learning, except for emphasising the necessity of preparation (see Chapter 3), and setting out the practical requirements of two different experiences over at least 200 days in total and involving statutory tasks. The criteria to note are contained within the National Occupational Standards, the social work subject benchmarks and social work values. Each university will have developed different specific criteria for assessing practice and this may be set at different levels depending on whether this is your first, second or, in some cases, third practice learning opportunity. However, assessment will ultimately test the same standards. Figure 5.2 sets out the key standards and requirements to be met.

Of course, the standards go into much greater detail and you should become familiar with the units as this will help you to link your practice to them. The complete set of standards and units are shown in Figure 5.3.

---

*Key Role 1:* **Prepare for and work with individuals, families, carers, groups and communities to assess their needs and circumstances**

- Prepare for social work contact and involvement

- Work with individuals, families, carers, groups and communities to help them make informed decisions

- Assess needs and options to recommend a course of action

*Key Role 2:* **Plan, carry out, review and evaluate social work practice, with individuals, families, carers, groups and communities and other professionals**

- Respond to crisis situations

- Interact with individuals, families, carers, groups and communities to achieve change and development and to improve life opportunities

- Prepare, produce, implement and evaluate plans with individuals, families, carers, groups, communities and professional colleagues

- Support the development of networks to meet assessed needs and planned outcomes

- Work with groups to promote individual growth, development and independence

- Address behaviour which presents a risk to individuals, families, carers, groups, communities

*Key Role 3:* **Support individuals to represent their needs, views and circumstances**

- Advocate with and on behalf of, individuals, families, carers, groups and communities

- Prepare for, and participate in decision making forums

*Key Role 4:* **Manage risk to individuals, families, carers, groups, communities, self and colleagues**

- Assess and manage risks to individuals, families, carers, groups and communities

- Assess, minimise and manage risk to self and colleagues

*Key Role 5:* **Manage and be accountable, with supervision and support, for your own social work practice within your organisation**

- Manage and be accountable for your own work

- Contribute to the management of resources and services

---

**Figure 5.3** *The National Occupational Standards for Social Work (TopssEngland, 2002)*

- Manage, present and share records and reports

- Work within multi-disciplinary and multi-organisational teams, networks and system

*Key Role 6:* **Demonstrate professional competence in social work practice**

- Research, analyse, evaluate and use current knowledge of best social work practice

- Work within agreed standards of social work practice and ensure own professional development

- Manage complex ethical issues, dilemmas and conflicts

- Contribute to the promotion of best social work practice

*Figure 5.3* (continued)

The standards and units are not prescriptive. They are constructed in ways that allow them to be defined more precisely in each practice learning opportunity. For instance, to meet the unit 'respond to crisis situations' from Key Role 2 in a day-care setting for older people may be assessed by considering how you respond when the transport does not turn up, what procedures you follow and how you deal with irate relatives and carers. In a child-care team for looked-after children, this may relate to working in a situation in which a foster placement has reached the point of breakdown. It will be up to you and your practice teacher to determine learning opportunities to meet the standards and requirements, and then for you to collect and present evidence of having achieved them that can be scrutinised and assessed by your practice teacher.

---

*ACTIVITY* **5.1**

*Take another unit from the National Occupational Standards and apply this to your practice learning setting. What evidence will you use, which case examples and what ways of working? Think about the evidence you chose and consider alternative ways of demonstrating that you have met this unit. Remember to examine the values and principles on which your practice was based.*

---

It can be tempting to concentrate on meeting the above standards and to push other aspects of your learning to the sidelines. However, practice learning goes much deeper than achieving a standard and moving on to the next; it relates to learning to practise in very complex and challenging human situations. To practise effectively and ethically, you need to work from a secure value base. We explored some of the values underpinning practice learning in Chapter 1 and you should revisit this at this point.

## Quality assurance and the assessment process

Practice learning opportunities need to be 'fit for purpose', that is they need to offer you the learning opportunities to meet the standards and requirements for social work practice. You can begin the process, or at least prepare for it, when you negotiate your practice learning agreement and identify opportunities and objectives which will enhance your knowledge and skills and assist in meeting some of the standards. However, practice learning needs to provide adequate opportunities and it is important that you are able to assess the worth of the learning opportunity for other student social workers. No doubt your university will have in place its own audit and quality assurance systems that will seek your views concerning the experience. You should be honest and open in your responses. Sometimes students feel uneasy about responding negatively to aspects of a practice learning opportunity. This may be more the case if feedback is not anonymous or is sought before the end of the practice learning opportunity. However, it is in the interests of the university, the practice agency, the social work profession and, most importantly, of service users that practice learning prepares you for social work practice and constructive criticism is generally welcomed. The Practice Learning Taskforce has developed a tool for collecting feedback electronically that may also help in preserving anonymity. You can find an example of this Practice Learning Quality Evaluation Tool at **www.practicelearning.org.uk/pelqet/index.htm**.

Some universities have maintained their practice assessment or practice evaluation panels, a quality assurance system that was developed for the previous qualification. Panels comprise members from the university and from practice agencies. While these systems generally consider at least a sample of evidence from practice learning, they are also interested in assessing the quality of the experiences and learning opportunities offered and also the work of practice teachers in supporting and assessing students.

The emphasis on quality assurance is helpful and should provide you with a degree of security in practice learning.

It is your learning and practice that is assessed during practice learning. The assessment will be tailored to your specific agency or practice base but is likely to focus on the National Occupational Standards and the value base of social work. The university will want also to ensure that the subject benchmark criteria are addressed. While it is your practice teacher who will make the final assessment, you too will be involved in collecting and presenting evidence. The production of the self-evaluation report and what this communicates will be dealt with in Chapter 6, but in the next section we will consider what evidence is and how you might demonstrate it in your practice learning.

# Evidence in the assessment process

## What is evidence?

When we begin to talk about evidence, it is quite likely that a range of understandings come to mind. One of these may relate to popular conceptions of evidence taken from courtroom or police dramas in which evidence relates to the material facts of the case. However, evidence is often not so clear-cut and it may involve a degree of interpretation of what happened, the facts of which may not be fully known. Evidence may be 'circumstantial', depending on an analysis of the facts without hard evidence to back the interpretation. This begins to show some of the complexities and issues that arise in using evidence which apply to social work practice and, in your case, to the use of evidence in assessing your competence to practise.

The term 'evidence-based practice' is central to the development of contemporary social work. D'Cruz and Jones (2004) suggest that this may be understood as irrefutable evidence of effectiveness of certain types of practice and provides credibility for the social work profession. However, questions need to be considered as to whether a comprehensive evidence base can be generated to inform practice and who decides what constitutes evidence. D'Cruz and Jones (2004) believe that the political and ethical aspects involved in generating evidence must be taken into account when assessing it.

Wherever possible an assessment in practice learning should be evidenced-based. It should be able to show the facts relating to your practice and link these to specific criteria for assessment. However, it is recognised that there will necessarily be a degree of interpretation in the assessment, especially when applying a judgement concerning how well a task is performed. This indicates that there is an unequal power balance in the relationship between yourself and your practice teacher who is responsible for developing these interpretations and in turn making a recommendation concerning your suitability to your university. This aspect of the relationship should be openly acknowledged.

## How do you gather and demonstrate evidence?

Even where your evidence at first sight seems clear and based on actions, roles and tasks that you have undertaken, there is a degree of interpretation involved in linking it to specific standards in the assessment. Your university practice team will no doubt have offered you some guidance on gathering and using evidence but you may find the following hints helpful.

You should seek to gather evidence from a wide range of sources. These may include:

- letters, case records, reports;
- notes relating to presentations made to team meetings or colleagues;
- feedback from colleagues on presentations made;
- feedback from colleagues on work undertaken in the office or jointly on visits;
- observations of practice;
- discussions within supervision;
- feedback from service users and carers;
- a work record;
- reflective journal or diary.

The evidence should be related to specific learning objectives and it is helpful to discuss the process within supervision. One question that concerns many students – and, indeed, qualified social workers – is: 'How do I know the evidence is appropriate?' It is useful to check your evidence against the following criteria:

- *Is it valid?* Does the evidence relate specifically to a requirement included in the practice learning agreement and does it demonstrate use of agency policy, procedure and practice?
- *Is it sufficient?* Has the evidence been seen frequently enough to justify the assessment and is it of sufficient depth?
- *Is it relevant?* Does the evidence relate specifically to the standard being considered or does it cover it in part or not at all?
- *Is it based in social work values?* Does it reflect anti-oppressive values and promote a value-based approach to social work?

- *Is it reliable?* Does the evidence build a consistent picture when taken together with other evidence from a range of sources?

- *Is it clear?* Can the description of the evidence and the evidence itself be understood by others to relate to an assessed objective?

- *Is it agreed?* Has the relevance and interpretation of the evidence been agreed by all involved – yourself as student, practice teacher, colleagues, service users and carers?

---

### ACTIVITY 5.2

Considering the criteria above, return to the extract from Petra's learning agreement in Chapter 3 and review the evidence in the following case study.

---

### CASE STUDY

I have shown that I have met units 2 to 5 of Key Role 2 in my work with the 'I'm not alone' group. I spent ten weeks of my practice learning opportunity working with the group and have led four of the sessions. I planned my work carefully, listening to the wishes of the group in exploring homelands and journeys to England. I evaluated each session by asking members for feedback and giving everyone a feedback form (although only a handful were returned).

Towards the end of the group work we found out about other groups and clubs in the area, made contact with them and went to visit a local disco and a mixed football club.

My colleague, PJ, who ran the group with me, has provided feedback on my work.

---

### ACTIVITY 5.2 (continued)

This is only a short extract of Petra's self-evaluation and when finally presented it would be more comprehensive and detailed. However, it provides a useful example to consider validity and relevance against the original learning agreement and the key roles of the National Occupational Standards: sufficiency, reliability and clarity. It would have helped Petra if she had emphasised more fully the values demonstrated in this piece of work. She mentions following the lead of the group members and checking things out with them but does not explicitly link this to social work values or the Code of Practice.

---

In Chapter 1 you were introduced to a model of assessment that suggested you collect evidence throughout practice learning and check this out before using it in your final assessment. The model also suggested using reflection as a way of identifying learning and developing plans to continue your development throughout (see Figure 1.5). You should keep in mind formative, summative and reflective assessment as you work through this chapter, asking yourself the following questions:

- What aspects of my learning can I check with my practice teacher or assessor?

- What evidence will contribute to my final assessment and how might I present this effectively?

- What learning can I take forward into new situations?

# Assessment and the self

## Can you assess yourself?

There is an ongoing debate within higher education as a whole that questions whether students can comment on assessment practice and quality and, therefore, whether students are able to assess themselves adequately. In terms of the quality of assessment the criterion of 'fitness for purpose' – or does it test what it purports to test – holds good.

Most universities assess student satisfaction on teaching and learning issues but may not pay as much attention to assessment because it is assumed that:

- students are not sufficiently knowledgeable about assessment to comment;

- students may not recognise or assess appropriately the purpose of assessment;

- since students are being judged or tested their views are not sufficiently objective (McDowell and Sambell, 1999).

In McDowell and Sambell's case study research, however, it was found that students prefer assessment to be interesting and challenging as a vehicle for learning rather than easy to pass. What students did want in assessment is to be engaged in the learning process, to receive feedback to enhance future learning and to know clearly what is expected. These are important issues for practice learning in which you, as the student, will play a part. This small study also shows that students are able to assess themselves. In practice learning self-assessment in the form of a critical evaluation of learning is fairly common as a constituent part of the process.

Self-assessment alone is not appropriate in practice learning but may form one useful method among the range of stakeholders involved (see Erwin, 1991). We have considered self-assessment when debating reflective practice in Chapter 2. Using the tools described there, such as keeping a reflective journal or constructing narratives or critical incident reports will help you to form a judgement of how you are progressing in your practice learning. Shared with your practice teacher this can be instrumental in furthering your development, especially in identifying learning needs.

## Gathering evidence from colleagues

Most practice learning occurs in teams comprising social workers or other professionals and workers. Your colleagues are a valuable resource to be tapped into for evidence for assessment. Your practice teacher will want to seek the views of people you work with and it can be helpful for you to do so.

Some of your colleagues may have an assessment function and contribute to the formal process but it is most likely that the majority will offer feedback on specific pieces of work or in general terms about your practice and behaviour in the workplace. Seeking the feedback of colleagues can be daunting, as, indeed, can giving it. You must be prepared and ask for honest feedback. It is only relevant and useful if it is accurate. While it might be comfortable to give or receive positive feedback and potentially upsetting to receive criticism, the latter can assist you in identifying issues within your practice that need further work and development.

Your colleagues may be involved in observing your practice directly and feedback from these sessions can contribute to your development as well as to your overall assessment. An example of a feedback form for direct practice used by the Universities of Hull and Lincoln is shown in Figure 5.4.

---

**DIRECT OBSERVATION FORM**

Name of student:

Name of observer:

Date of observation:

Event observed:

---

Comment on how the student prepared for the session:

Comment on the student's communication skills:

How did the student demonstrate values in their practice?

How far did the student meet their objectives?

How did they respond to unanticipated events (if any)?

Comment on the student's overall performance:

Student's response to the feedback:

Signed:

Date:

---

**Figure 5.4**  *Example of a feedback form for direct practice*

# Assessment and feedback from service users and carers

Kearney (2003, p4), in the SCIE position paper on supporting and assessing practice learning in the new degree, sets the context for assessment by service users by stressing the 'primacy of service users' experiences and on understanding and experience of collaborative working with other professions'.

Thomas (2002) describes a small project concerning the involvement of service users in the assessment of student practice learning. This was based on a Midland Regional Conference for Practice Teachers held in 1999. Sixty practice teachers and tutors were involved in one of six workshops that considered three scenarios designed to stimulate thinking about how service users might be involved in student assessment and what issues might arise. Following the workshop an issues paper was circulated to participants to continue thinking about this issue. Two clear points were raised initially that indicated clear criteria for assessment or feedback were needed and that using a specific tool designed to assist service users in giving feedback would be helpful. These points are ones that you could usefully bear in mind when seeking feedback from service users as part of your own assessment or when encouraging involvement in the assessment process. Of course, your university will have a particular way of involving service users and carers in gathering feedback on or assessing your practice and this will guide the way you seek the views of service users and carers. However, it is extremely helpful to hone your knowledge, skills and values in practice by systematically collecting feedback from service users throughout practice learning. If you are to do this, you need to be clear, honest and open with service users concerning what you want feedback on, what the information will be used for and provide assurances that the feedback concerns your development and is not a precondition for a service. There are issues of power and ethics that need to be addressed in collecting feedback from service users and carers but this should not become an excuse for avoiding this very useful component to the assessment of your practice learning.

The issues paper developed after the workshops in Thomas's (2002) research considered three particular areas affecting service users' involvement in assessment or giving feedback on students' practice learning:

- *competence* – the ability to give reasoned arguments that matched practice to set and agreed outcomes;

- *fairness* – which concerned the right of service users to make comments based on observed evidence without fear or favour, and the range of comments to be extensive enough not to unjustly affect the student's overall assessment;

- *training and methods* – procedures and processes should be established to prepare people about the role and remit of feedback and/or assessment.

There is still little 'specifically written about service user involvement in student assessment' (Thomas, 2002, p36; see also Shardlow and Doel, 1996, and Edwards, 2003). Thomas asks the questions whether or not it is a good idea to involve service users in the assessment of practice, why should we do it, and what is its purpose? If it is about empowerment and giving people a voice then he argues that such feedback or assessment should be extended to all employees of the agency and should become part of its ethos. This suggestion accords well with the developing emphasis on service user and carer involvement at all levels of practice, education and training. This is perhaps a debate for your practice teacher and agency staff to have but it is an important point in recognising the centrality of equitable treatment and fair play.

Another question asked is whether or not service users should be expected to give feedback about a student and his or her practice or whether they should be involved in the assessment itself. This is an important question and one which your university will no doubt have grappled with and formulated some guidelines for your overall assessment of practice. However, to enhance the effectiveness of your practice learning the emphasis should be on how you might seek feedback to improve and develop your practice, who you might seek that feedback from and how you should use it. Constructing a pro forma set of questions, structured or semi-structured, may be one way of achieving this. Furniss (1988) suggests a structured approach using the practice teacher as interviewer. However, it is valuable to collect this information yourself, bearing in mind the power issues between yourself and service users and the importance of the principle of 'fairness' referred to above. It is fundamental that service users do not think they have to provide feedback to gain a service and, even more so, that they do not feel they have to provide positive feedback rather than an honest appraisal. Indeed, it is more important for your own development and learning to receive open, critical feedback. While we would no doubt all prefer any critical feedback received to be constructive, we cannot necessarily assume this will be the case. In order to use feedback to enhance your practice, you should seek to share it with your practice teacher in a developmental way. This can provide you with support and can assist you in facing up to negative views that you might wish to dismiss.

## Grasping the nettle and finding solutions

It may be possible to use a feedback sheet to assist service users and carers in giving feedback. However, this is only relevant where service users are able to complete such forms and this is not always the case. You may be able to ask a set of questions that would help to elicit feedback but service users and carers may not wish to say anything negative in your presence. To use a third party, perhaps your practice teacher, would possibly get around this problem but would remove you from the situation.

Thomas (2002) provided a set of principles that are useful in guiding the involvement of service users in giving feedback and these principles are important for you to adopt in negotiating any feedback to be given. First, service users must be afforded the right to clear information about what might be expected of them and how they might be involved as well as the right not to be involved. If service users are to give feedback, they should be able to identify and set areas about which to make comments. Also, an agreement should be reached between practice teacher and student to select and ask service users for feedback and a range of ways of making comments should be explored.

The areas you want to gain information on include some of the following:

- your attitude and approach;

- your punctuality;

- the clarity of your information giving;

- whether you did what you said you would;

- the degree to which you respected service user and carer wishes;

- whether they were generally satisfied with you and your work;

- whether there are aspects of your work and approach they would like to change;

- anything else they might wish to comment on in respect of your involvement.

---

CASE STUDY

*James had been working with Jane concerning her substance use and the potential risks to her young children when she was using. In seeking feedback on the work, Jane expressed a high degree of satisfaction, stating that he always turned up and did whatever had been agreed during the previous session. However, she said that she thought the sessions were confidential between James and herself and had not expected James to share things with his practice teacher. Fortunately, this did not lead to any problems arising and James was able to explain again the policy on confidentiality and its limits. What this feedback did raise was that James needed to be much clearer and explicit when explaining agency policies to service users.*

---

# What happens when things go wrong

Assessment is the culmination of your practice learning experience and you will wish to pass. Events do not always run smoothly, however, and some people do not progress through the assessment stage. For some people this comes as a welcome release when they realise they do not wish to practise as a social worker. For many it is more painful. Your university will detail its process and procedure for dealing with 'failing' practice learning opportunities and you should make yourself aware of it. In Chapter 1, we covered some of the options available to you in making a complaint should this be warranted or in making an appeal, generally against procedures not being followed and not against the decision. We also outlined issues of professional suitability that must be preserved during practice learning.

If things go wrong on practice, you should be informed as soon as possible. We often learn from our mistakes and from situations of tension and conflict. So a problem during the practice learning opportunity is not necessarily the beginning of the end but an opportunity to develop new knowledge and skills and to demonstrate development. One way of assisting yourself through the process is to continue to collect good evidence, using the criteria set out earlier in the chapter and a formative, summative and reflective approach (see Figure 1.5). It is fundamental to your learning to make an honest appraisal of yourself. This will help in demonstrating your commitment to the process and help both you and your practice teacher to refine or revise your practice learning agreement to meet your needs.

## C H A P T E R   S U M M A R Y

In this chapter, we have considered the assessment of practice learning in relation to the standards expected and the quality of evidence to be gathered and presented. We have considered the importance of self-assessment and seeking feedback from colleagues and service users. We have not considered the assessment from the perspective of the practice teacher as, in many ways, the evidence you collect and especially the self-evaluation report you produce (see Chapter 6) is likely to form the basis of the practice teacher's assessment. A key characteristic of the assessment of practice learning should be that it is a collaborative process in which you play a valuable part. In the next chapter, we will consider the production of your self-assessment report but will do so in the context of the communication skills that are integral to effective practice learning.

*FURTHER READING*

There is no specific recommended reading for this chapter except to refer you back to your course or programme documentation which will detail what you have to do, and should provide you with hints and suggestions as to how you might go about the process of collecting evidence and making a self-assessment.

# Chapter 6

## Developing skills and communicating effectively

This chapter will help you to meet the following National Occupational Standards:

**Key Role 5: Manage and be accountable, with supervision and support, for your own social work practice within your organisation**

- Manage and be accountable for your own work
- Contribute to the management of resources and services
- Manage, present and share records and reports
- Work within multi-disciplinary and multi-organisational teams, networks and systems

**Key Role 6: Demonstrate professional competence in social work practice**

- Research, analyse, evaluate and use current knowledge of best social work practice
- Work within agreed standards of social work practice and ensure own professional development
- Manage complex ethical issues, dilemmas and conflicts
- Contribute to the promotion of best social work practice.

It will also introduce you to the following academic standards as set out in the social work subject benchmark statement:

**3.2.1 Communication and IT skills**

**3.2.2 Problem-solving skills**

- Manage problem-solving activities
- Gather information
- Analyse and synthesise information
- Intervene and evaluate practice

**3.2.2 Communication skills**

- Good oral and written communication skills
- Make effective contact with a range of people for a range of reasons
- Clarify and negotiate purpose and boundaries
- Listen, engage, understand and reflect; overcome personal prejudices to respond
- Verbal and non-verbal cues
- Identify and use opportunities for purposeful and supportive communication in everyday life situations of service users
- Follow and develop argument, evaluate views and evidence of others
- Write accurately and appropriately for purpose
- Present structured conclusions verbally and on paper
- Prepare and lead meetings
- Communicate effectively across potential barriers

**3.2.4 Skills in working with others**

- Develop effective relationships and partnerships.

# Introduction

Following on from Chapter 5, this chapter will explore some of the skills to be developed to show competent practice. These skills will include interpersonal communication between yourself and service users and carers, with colleagues in the practice agency and with other professionals and agencies. The skills examined will go deeper, however, than interpersonal communication involving direct contact between yourself and another person and will look at ways of communicating effectively using the telephone and writing letters and professional reports. An important part of this chapter will consider some of the communication skills needed for compiling and presenting an effective self-evaluation report showing the learning that has taken place and the evidence on which you judge the practice learning experience and your future learning needs. This will include an examination of what might go into a self-evaluation or self-assessment report and what standards it should be written against. It is important that we understand communication as being much more than the spoken or heard words of another. This chapter will help you identify a range of different ways of communicating, all of which are important in effective practice learning. Simplicity and clarity are key principles to maintain at all times.

# Using interpersonal skills in practice learning

The importance of being 'able to communicate clearly and accurately in spoken and written English' (Department of Health, 2002, p2) forms part of the entry requirements for the social work degree and, by being on your programme, you will already have been judged to have at least a basic level of skill. However, learning is not static and it is during practice learning that the skills of communication are put fully to the test.

You will communicate with and use your interpersonal skills in many situations in the course of practice learning. You will speak with, listen to and forge a working collaborative relationship with your practice teacher or assessor, with other colleagues within your practice agency and with other professionals outside the practice agency. You will communicate using verbal and non-verbal interpersonal skills with service users and their carers and will, at times, be expected to present your role and profession to the general public. Many of the interpersonal skills that you might use are similar but applied differently according to each particular situation or setting. Some are specific to the location in which you find yourself.

Communication is a complex phenomenon. We may have a 'common-sense' view that communication relates to how we speak to and listen to one another. However, it is deeper than this. At a simple level, 'communication concerns interacting with another and involves giving, receiving, interpreting and acting upon or responding to information' (Parker, 2003, p149). While the two key skills involved in communicating are generally recognised as talking and listening, we communicate by our body language and posture and in non-verbal ways. We communicate visually, by touch and in written and/or electronic form, and we communicate something about ourselves, and our understanding of the world, by the jobs we do and the ways in which we do them. One interesting method of communication, and one that requires highly developed skills to work with, is not

responding when a person tries to communicate in some way. Sometimes this is deliberate, sometimes it sends the message that the person not responding is overloaded or too
busy, or it may suggest that the person trying to communicate is 'not worth the effort'
which can be very disconcerting.

Figure 6.1 provides a visual display of some of the ways in which we communicate.

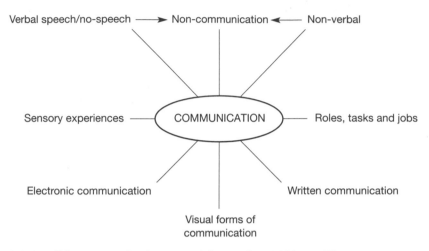

**Figure 6.1** *Possible communication types (after Parker, 2003, p149)*

All these forms of communication are useful in the practice learning experience and you
need to develop skills in using them all.

Traditional forms of communication theory 'examine the processes that communication
involves: the selection of a means of conveying a message (language, gesture, writing),
the decoding of the message by the recipient (hearing, seeing, reading), and making a
response on the basis of the interaction (reply)' (Randall and Parker, 2000, p69).

# Interpersonal communication – in person and on the telephone

While you can gain a good introduction to interpersonal communication in Koprowska
(2004), it is important to revisit some of the basic conditions for effective communication
and some of the core skills you will be expected to use during your practice learning
opportunities.

## Communication skills

The core conditions for effective interpersonal communication with others are well known
(Parker and Bradley, 2003). It is important to step into the world of the person you are
engaging with and to test your understanding by paraphrasing and reflecting what has
been said and what you believe has been expressed emotionally (empathy). This will help

you convey respect for the other person (warmth) as will being open, honest and clear (genuineness) in your reasons for communicating with a person, family or group. These conditions of empathy, warmth and genuineness are enhanced by being specific and focused on present concerns and issues while picking up and testing discrepancies.

These conditions will help you to establish a relationship but in order to communicate effectively you will need to pay attention to micro-skills such as how and where you sit with respect to the person you are communicating with, whether you cross your legs, fold your arms or lean towards the person and how much eye contact to make. Listening to and being aware of your body language and that of the person you are talking with is also important. You need to consider:

* bodily movement or how people fidget and wriggle;

* facial expressions such as smiles, raised eyebrows;

* the tone, volume and quality of speech – is it slow, loud, does it wobble?

* does the person blush, develop a reddening of the neck, do pupils dilate?

Many of the above characteristics are highlighted when dealing with interpersonal communication. However, it is important to remember that there are significant social and cultural differences in the way people act when communicating with another person. Also, if you are too rigid in maintaining an open posture and calm voice when you do not usually do so you run the risk of putting off the person you are engaged with. The best advice in using and developing interpersonal skills is two-fold: know yourself and be yourself!

---

*ACTIVITY* **6.1**

*Engaging in communication with another person demands quite a significant understanding of yourself and the way you present when interacting with another person. This may change according to the role you are playing at the time. Think back to a recent social meeting with a friend or family member. Identify how you spoke with that person, how you presented and used your body language and how the conversation developed. Now do the same for a meeting between yourself and a practice colleague or another student. Highlight the similarities and differences in approach.*

*If you are unsure about how you used your communication skills and body language, repeat the activity consciously in your next meetings. This may make you rather self-conscious and you should inform and seek the permission of the person you are interacting with first. However, this may help you identify important aspects of the way you use yourself in communication with others. Do not be too concerned if you did not follow a textbook example of how to communicate. Remember: be yourself.*

---

During your practice learning opportunities you are likely to communicate directly with a range of individuals in different ways. The most common will include using interpersonal skills:

* to communicate with service users;

* to communicate with carers;

- to communicate with colleagues;

- to communicate with other professionals and other agencies;

- in group and meeting settings.

It is important in all the above situations that you consider issues of power and role as this may influence the direction and flow of the discussion. For instance, when talking with another professional you will be conscious of the need for confidentiality, what information can be shared and what cannot. This may lead you to be firm in stating that you cannot talk about a certain issue. When you discuss this with your practice teacher and he or she asks you to explain the reasons behind your communication to that professional you will be conscious that the practice teacher is assessing your performance and levels of competence and will want to ensure that he or she knows you are progressing appropriately.

When communicating in groups, the interpersonal skills mentioned remain important. However, you need to be aware that there are a range of other interactions and dynamics that can affect communication in group settings (see below).

## Characterisics of groups

There is a range of special features and characteristics in groups that it is essential to bear in mind when planning and running groups as a medium to help people.

Groups develop particular moods and atmospheres from within the membership of the group. These moods may develop from single incidents but may affect everyone involved and these shared themes may preoccupy a group for some time.

Groups evolve norms and belief systems. Norms are common or shared beliefs that shape the behaviour and attitudes of group members. They may be expressed quite forcefully on occasions.

Group members might occupy different positions within the group in terms of power, centrality, being liked or disliked but these can change throughout the course of the group. They are generally associated with a position in which the person feels safe. Members of a group may, however, jostle for comfortable positions and form alliances and collude with others to achieve this.

Individuals sometimes find one or two others to whom they are especially close or find particularly important to them. They share some similarities with people significant to them or aspects of themselves.

The following case study indicates some of the issues involved in communicating with others. It may seem complex, but remember you are using skills that you use unconsciously in your daily life. When using them in practice learning, you are transferring the everyday to a particular setting.

---

**CASE STUDY**

*Tom asked Margot where she would like him to sit after remembering that she pulled him up quite abruptly when he sat in her late husband's chair during the last visit. He sat facing her and explained the reason for this visit while asking her if she had any questions about this, checking that she understood why he was there. Tom needed to collect more information about her social circumstances, friends and help in the neighbourhood as part of an assessment of need for personal care. He sat forward, listening intently as she spoke and asked, on a couple of occasions, if he could jot down some notes. Tom was conscious throughout that Margot had a hearing impairment and he wanted to ensure that she had heard and understood him. He was careful not to shout but spoke clearly, with his hand away from his face and checked, at regular intervals, what had been said.*

*On returning to the office, Tom had to discuss the visit with his practice teacher. His practice teacher wanted him to explain the purpose for the visit, the legislation relevant to the visit, what went according to plan and what he had learned to take into the future. Tom felt confident that the visit had proceeded well and was able to deal with the practice teacher's questions. However, he learned from the experience that there is a significant difference between leading an interview and being on the receiving end. The importance of creating a relaxed and friendly environment was reinforced.*

## Using the telephone

Social workers, as we have noted, communicate with many people, about many varied and different issues, using a wide range of different ways of doing so. The telephone is certainly one of the most widely used ways of communicating and during your practice learning experiences you will be expected to use the telephone to contact service users, carers and professionals in other teams or from different disciplines. You need, therefore, to develop you skills in using the telephone for professional communication. Using interpersonal skills on and communicating by the telephone can be very different to interacting with someone face to face. It can also be very different to using the telephone in everyday life.

**ACTIVITY 6.2**

*Make a list of some of the key difficulties that come to mind in using the telephone to communicate rather than speaking with someone face to face.*

You may have identified some of the following:

| What you cannot rely on | What you need to concentrate upon |
| --- | --- |
| You cannot see the person | You need to pay attention to tone and quality of speech |
| You cannot see body language | You need to consider pauses |
| You cannot see facial expression | You need to reflect back content |
| You do not necessarily know who else is there or what else might be happening around the person | You need to explore what you think might be happening for the person |
| | Reflect emotions you might pick up, for instance did the person tremble in their speech, were there any sobs, laughs and such like |

Using the telephone to communicate for professional purposes differs according to the purpose of the call and the person you are calling. Consider the following scenarios:

Jenny, a social work student, rang a neighbouring team in which her colleague, Tim, was undertaking his practice learning. She needed to arrange a case discussion. The conversation went as follows:

*Jane*: Hi Tim. How's it going?

*Tim*: Oh you know …

*Jane*: The team here's great. I'm getting lots of cases, and Reuben's [practice teacher] pretty cool. Anyway, I wanted to arrange a case discussion about Martin D.

*Tim*: Yeah, sure. When for?

This conversation flowed easily. The students knew each other and the conversation began with pleasantries before moving on to making arrangements. They were confident with one another but also able to get down to the purpose of the call.

Gillian had received a referral from a school nurse concerning a child's behavioural difficulties and suspected substance use. She was asked to telephone the child's mother to arrange a visit.

*Gillian*: Hello, is that Mrs E? Good. My name is Gillian Farr from social services.

*Mrs E*: Oh yes.

*Gillian*: I'm ringing about Tony …

*Mrs E*: Why? I had the school nurse on earlier saying you might call, it's not like he's abused or something. I don't know why you're ringing …

*Gillian*: Yes, I spoke with the school nurse earlier and it's about Tony's behaviour that I'm ringing. I'd like to arrange a visit if poss …

*Mrs E*: I know he's a handful but I can't see why social services have to be involved. I don't want to lose him you know.

*Gillian:* I realise it must be very confusing having different people ring and I do think it would be better to meet to discuss things. Social services aren't just about taking people into care and our team works to support families in looking after children …

This call was more difficult for the student and she had to think quickly and carefully about what she might say. She wanted to reassure Mrs E that she was not acting in a child protection capacity but quite rightly did not promise that Tony would not be taken into care because the future can never be so clearly anticipated. She also tried to explain the role of the team and purpose of the visit. She did not mention substance use over the telephone because this was suspected rather than known and she made the decision to be there to support Mrs E when she brought it up. Gillian tried to reflect some of the confusion and uncertainty expressed by Mrs E.

---

**ACTIVITY 6.3**

*Think of the purposes you might use the telephone for as a social worker and make a list of these.*

*In drawing up your list, you may have identified some of the following:*

- *making initial contact with a person referred to your agency;*

- *contacting another professional who has made a referral to your agency;*

- *contacting another professional or agency to gather information about someone you are working with (bearing in mind the need to have service user permission and also the need to protect data and confidentiality);*

- *contacting people to arrange or rearrange visits;*

- *arranging meetings;*

- *ensuring people are 'on track' with tasks set between visits;*

- *as a means of showing interest and support to someone you're working with;*

- *as a means of organising services;*

- *making a referral to another agency.*

*This list is not exhaustive and there may be many more possible reasons for using the telephone that you have identified. What is important is that you will be using the telephone as a student social worker undertaking practice learning and you will need to be confident and assured in using this means of communication.*

---

It is common for students to find that the skills of using the telephone, which you will probably use on a daily basis for talking with friends and family, seem to disappear as soon as you are undertaking practice learning and being assessed in practice. There is a variety of ways that you can begin to re-establish and further develop confidence in using the telephone. We will review some of these now.

### Observing your practice teacher/other workers within the office

In the early days of your practice learning experience, you may have the opportunity to sit by and observe how your practice teacher and others in the team respond to telephone calls. This may provide you with ideas and examples that you could use.

### Role-play

If you are particularly nervous about using the telephone and you cannot use a separate room in which to practise, it can help if you act out a number of different but typical telephone conversations. This can be done with your practice teacher, with other colleagues or, indeed, with other students. If you are placed with other students or you have formed an action learning set (see Chapter 2), you might like to role-play a telephone call using one of the following scenarios or one that better fits your agency:

- a service user who wants some help with his alcohol consumption;
- a son who wants his mother with Alzheimer's disease placing in residential care;
- a father who wants increased contact with his son who lives with his mother and new partner who is known to social services;
- a GP who wants to refer someone for a benefit review;
- a police officer referring a family in which there is known domestic violence.

### Writing plans of things to say

Whatever you are doing, it can be helpful to construct a plan of action. This works equally well in making telephone calls. Think about the reason for your call and what you hope to achieve. Consider likely reactions and identify how you will deal with these. Write down some key notes including:

- aim of call;
- agency information to provide;
- specific information to provide;
- outcomes to achieve.

These will help you keep on track. It is also useful to use a written plan to assess how far the call met its stated aims, what differed from the plan and why that might be.

Using a reflective journal (see Chapter 2) will provide you with some means of analysing the use of the telephone and exploring ways of improving your use.

## Written and electronic communication

### Use of information and communication technology (ICT) skills

Although the Department of Health (2002) did not make achieving the European Computer Driving Licence (ECDL) a requirement for the social work degree, the GSCC emphasises the skills and knowledge to the point of seeking evidence of how competence is achieved to the level of the ECDL in each university's degree. Your own university will require you to gain, develop and be assessed in the use of ICT skills as part of your programme. While each social work programme is different, there are common skills to be learned in using ICT. These may include being able to use ICT for a range of purposes including data searches, gathering and research, using the Internet, the compilation of word-processed documents, spreadsheets and use of databases, and using e-mail to communicate with people. It is likely that these skills will become increasingly important to your practice learning experience.

In this section, you will be introduced to some of the ways you might use e-mail or compile information that can be used to design a web page to communicate information about your agency, its role and tasks.

E-mail communication is a common medium for exchanging information and is used widely by many people. However, not everyone has had opportunities to communicate in this way and it is worth covering some basics.

The first essential point to remember in using electronic communication in practice learning is that each organisation will have regulations, policies and procedures governing the use of e-mail and you must familiarise yourself with them. For instance, it is likely that, alongside strictures against using e-mail and the Internet for publishing, sending or receiving offensive material, you will only be allowed access to ICT facilities for work purposes. You will not be able to send personal messages. You will also have to ensure that whatever information is sent does not contravene data protection legislation and you should check with your practice teacher or supervisor in the agency about these regulations. If you do misuse e-mail or the Internet it is likely that the agency will seek to take some action against you, and it may invoke your university and programme professional unsuitability procedures. Be careful!

After negotiating the parameters set for using e-mail, you will need to become familiar with the systems and programmes used in your agency. Often, there will be an ICT worker who can provide basic training and information on the use of computers, the Internet and e-mail. There is usually someone in the team who will be willing to provide assistance that is more informal.

Once you are clear about the use of ICT, you will be able to consider how and under what circumstances or for what purposes e-mail should be used. E-mail is a useful way of:

- arranging and confirming meetings between professionals within your agency and outside your agency;
- communicating on key issues arising in a situation, so long as issues of confidentiality and data protection are attended to;
- keeping a communication flow between you, your university tutor and the practice agency.

E-mail is not, at present, commonly used for arranging appointments with service users or carers. There is, however, every reason to believe that it will become more frequently used in the future. If this happens, then it is imperative that you ensure any communication is recorded and stored appropriately.

If you are sending an e-mail for any of the above purposes what do you need to bear in mind? Firstly, consider who it is that you are communicating with. Is it just the main recipient of the message or are there other people who you need to copy into the e-mail. This will affect how you convey the information, which should be clear, accessible and easily understood.

While there are no universally agreed conventions used for sending an e-mail, it is possible to develop a clear and formal system based on written letters. It is probably best to avoid using 'text-like' messages, abbreviations and jargon as this can be easily misunderstood or may exclude people from the message. Consider the following questions when writing e-mails:

- With whom am I communicating?

- What is it that I want to say?

- What aspects of confidentiality and data protection must I consider in sending this message?

- How understandable or accessible is my communication?

- With whom do I need to share this information?

- How do I store or record the information?

- Have I followed agency guidelines?

A further way of communicating is via the development of a web page. This is a more specialised and potentially complex activity that may form part of a practice learning project. If you have the opportunity to be involved in such, the questions asked about e-mail will still apply. You will need, however, the support of a specialised person within the agency.

### Written skills

Written communication skills are central to effective social work practice. Unfortunately, social workers have been severely criticised for not keeping case records up to date or writing them accurately, precisely or in a non-judgemental way. The centrality of good record-keeping that involves clear written skills was stressed within the recommendations of the Climbié inquiry (Laming, 2003). Social work reports have been seen as ungrammatical and poorly punctuated. This matters when information is seen by other agencies or in formal settings such as case conferences or courts. Sometimes the problems result from social workers trying to be over-complex in their work and sometimes it is due to the lack of importance attached to written forms of communication. Rai (2004) believes, however, that the requirement for literacy-competent social workers masks the many different social and cultural uses of language and she would promote a 'social practice' approach to written skills which acknowledges that choices and roles are important factors in determining written style. It is indeed important to write with the audience in mind and to acknowledge your role at the time. However, this does not preclude the need for clear, appropriate forms of communication for specific purposes in social work practice. Written communication skills are central to good practice on behalf of and with service users and carers.

There are many guidelines and study books now available that can help you to develop effective written communication skills. Among the best are Graham Hopkins's books *Plain English for Social Services: A Guide to Better Communication* (1998a) and *The Write Stuff:*

*A Guide to Effective Writing in Social Care and Related Services* (1998b). You may also wish to consult some of the academic study texts which are useful in developing transferable written skills (see Redman, 2001).

Often when students begin practice learning they forget, or push to one side, the skills developed in constructing and presenting clear arguments in essays and coursework. On the other hand, before many students begin practice learning they will dismiss the importance of written style, grammar, punctuation and expression, complaining to university tutors that they wish to practise social work rather than excel academically. It is when you begin your practice learning that the skills learned in presenting a clear, coherent and sustained argument come to the fore.

There are some circumstances that cause anxiety and difficulties in written work which need to be considered. As more becomes known about dyslexia and as assessments become more available, it may be that you have a diagnosed dyslexia. If this has been assessed, you should have received a detailed report suggesting ways of developing your written style and tips for constructing reports and notes. These hold good in the workplace just as much as in the classroom. You should share any diagnosis you may have with your practice teacher then appropriate assistance can be given. Dyslexia is a recognised disability and help can be given to ensure that your written work meets the required standards of the agency in which you undertake your practice learning.

If you find you have lost confidence in how to communicate in written form, or you are unsure of the agency expectations or conventions, the first thing you must do is to speak with your practice teacher or agency supervisor. Find out what is expected of you in terms of written communication. Is there a case record sheet and set criteria for what is recorded, how is it recorded, when is it recorded and who might have access to it? Is there a standard letter style? Is there administrative support, someone to check your letters or to monitor them before they are sent? What is expected in respect of reports? Who receives reports and for what purposes are they compiled?

All the above information is important if you are to demonstrate your competence in written communication.

If it is your first practice learning experience it may help to look through some of the written information produced by other members of the team and to analyse and comment on it. Ask the following questions of written material that you see:

- Is it understandable?

- Is the language simple?

- Are the aims clear?

- Does it follow agency guidelines?

- What would I do differently and what would I do the same?

Of course, you will need to be guided by your practice teacher on this activity and remain sensitive to other people's work.

Following an examination of the work of others, it is often helpful to write a letter to a fictitious service user to arrange an appointment or to compile a case report and chronology on the basis of an existing case.

---

**ACTIVITY 6.4**

*Write a letter to a service user confirming an arrangement to visit. In the letter explain the purpose of your visit, what your agency offers and the details of your visit, such as time, date and likely duration.*

*Write a second letter to the GP who referred the service user to you. Think about what information you should include.*

*Check these letters against your agency policy and procedure and share them with your practice teacher or a colleague in the office to gain further feedback.*

---

These activities are useful processes of learning and provide a safe means of testing your skills in practice. You will probably find that many agencies include activities akin to this as part of their practice curriculum if they have one (see Chapter 3).

# Assessing communication skills

It is helpful to see the practice learning experience as being about constructive assessment of your skills, knowledge and values. One of the best ways of assessing your learning is to use the 'abducted by aliens test', which asks the question, 'If you were abducted by aliens tomorrow would someone else in the office or agency be able to pick up your work and understand it?' If you can answer 'yes' your skills are developing well and you should identify what your strengths are and apply them to other aspects of your practice learning. If, on the other hand, you have to answer 'no' – which, if the test is undertaken honestly, will be the case for most people initially – you should identify what is letting you down and how you might improve it. Go back over some of the previous activities if there are aspects of written communication that you need to improve.

In general, however, you should subject your interpersonal, written and electronic communicating skills to the following evaluative questions:

• Did it achieve what you wanted to achieve?

• What worked well?

• What would you seek to improve or change?

Using a reflective approach to developing practice will help you enhance your communication. In the previous chapter, we discussed assessment in practice learning from a variety of sources, and seeking feedback from all those involved in your practice learning is important. Good assessment should include:

• self-assessment by considering what you have done, how you have practised and the effects of your practice;

- assessment by others (colleagues/practice teacher) – verbal feedback, formal assessment of observed practice;

- feedback from service users.

## Preparing and writing the self-evaluation report: an exercise in skilled communication

The self-assessment report is an important tool in communicating your development and achievements in practice. It is something that should show what you have done, how you have done it, what you have learned from the experience and what 'gaps' or needs you have identified from the experience for future practice learning. In preparing the report you should bear in mind the following:

- Gather evidence and check with your practice teacher and others – use a wide range of sources.

- Use interim reports to monitor your development in practice.

- Follow the guidance given by your university and by your practice teacher and practice learning agency.

- Check that the evidence you are using meets the guidelines set by your university.

- Write simply and clearly.

Each programme will have its own style but it is likely that you will be expected to record clear evidence describing what you have done, reflecting on it for your development and linking this to the standards and requirements set for your practice learning opportunity. The following example shows part of a completed self-assessment relating to Key Role 2.1:

| Key Role 2: Work with individuals, families, carers, groups and communities to help them make informed decisions | Date | Signature |
|---|---|---|
| 2.1 Inform individuals, families, carers, groups and communities about your own and the organisation's duties and responsibilities | 2 June 2005 | |

*I have worked with ten families during my practice learning opportunity, for seven of which I did the first visit. I always took a copy of the 'access to files' policy and the 'confidentiality' policy to first visits with service users. For example, with BP, I explained that I was from Greentrees Day Care and talked a little about what that was. He was already aware of this from a friend who attends*

> *and I thought it was beneficial for him to tell me what he knew about the centre then I could fill any gaps and also introduce the policies to him in a more natural way. I also told him about the daily charge for transport and meals. BP did not seem too keen on this and wanted to brush the issue aside, but I returned to it to check that he had understood.*
>
> *My experience has taught me that being prepared is important and that people appreciate having full information. In my future practice, I will aim to continue to provide full information. This will involve me in preparing my own knowledge of the service I am working in, how to access it and what it offers, and what information has been produced for service users.*

It is often the case that students get caught out by time and, not having continuously collected evidence throughout their practice learning, are faced with a tremendously exacting task of writing a self-evaluation report in a very short period of time at the end of the practice opportunity. Not only is this likely to lead to a poorly produced and evidenced self-assessment of learning, it is unnecessary. If you follow the suggestions and guidelines made throughout this book, you should be able to marshal and refine your evidence throughout practice learning and check this with your practice teacher and assessor. This evidence can be used for further reflection or to show development in learning, and it can be used in the production of your report. Using the model introduced in Figure 1.5 you will have a range of formative evidence and reflections that can contribute to your summative assessed piece of work.

## C H A P T E R   S U M M A R Y

This chapter has examined the central role of communication skills in practice learning and introduced you to some of the ways in which you might be expected to communicate. It has also provided some tips for enhancing your competence in communicating with others.

Effective communication with service users and carers and with colleagues, other professionals, your practice teacher and university staff is essential for your learning to evolve. These are skills that will transfer into qualified practice and cover a broad spectrum of methods, from the spoken and written to the electronic.

**FURTHER READING**

**Koprowska, J.** (2004) Interpersonal and Communication Skills in Social Work. Exeter: Learning Matters.
This simple and accessible text will provide you with an understanding of key concepts in communicating with others effectively in social work practice. It offers practical examples that can be used to enhance activities, discussion and tasks presented in this chapter.

**Thompson, N.** (2003) Communication and Language: A Handbook of Theory and Practice. Basingstoke: Palgrave Macmillan.
This is a more detailed and theoretical consideration of communication and language, how it is used in social work and potential meanings constructed within communication. It will provide you with important information and knowledge to enhance your academic performance and understanding.

# Chapter 7
## Tying it all together

Practice learning may be compared to a journey on which you progress, hopefully, to higher planes of learning and competence. However, although journeys come to an end, it is important to your future career and development that you see your learning in practice as something that should continue throughout your work as a social worker and not something that is simply to be passed.

Throughout this book, you have been introduced to a range of key aspects of practice learning in which you will need to be active in the pursuit of knowledge and skills. You will need to prepare appropriately, using your university documentation to check what you need to do, when you need to do it and how it should be done. You will be involved in supervision sessions, not as an empty vessel to be filled by the experience of others but as a participant who is involved in negotiating the agenda and identifying opportunities, experiences and resources to meet your learning needs. You will be party to an assessment of your skills and competence to practise and asked to contribute in no small part to that process.

All the above demand a high level of interpersonal skill and a clarity of communication to make your voice heard, to listen to others and to secure the best possible learning experiences. This is important because you are being educated in practice to work alongside people who have been socially excluded for a variety of reasons, and who have often been marginalised and oppressed by the ways in which society operates. Your skills need to be effective in making a difference for the people you work with and your experiences during your practice learning opportunities will contribute to this development.

I have spoken with many experienced social workers and social work educators and many have said that they can remember their practice learning opportunities when training as social workers but often have little memory of any other part of their programme. This is not because the programmes were in any way irrelevant or poorly thought of, it is because the practice experience is the place in which your knowledge comes to life and is used to effect change, both in yourself as a developing professional and within those with whom you practise.

You should spend a little time reflecting on the key themes of the book, your learning and how you might meet the six National Occupational Standards for social work and promote the values enshrined within the Code of Practice for social workers. This book can be used in a way that allows you to revisit aspects of practice learning. If there are elements of practice learning that you have found difficult or need to enhance you can return to individual chapters or single activities. The important thing to remember is that your learning contributes to your development as a professional and skilled social worker who works effectively with service users and carers. The ways in which you manage and develop your learning will be, to some extent, unique to you.

# References

Beatty, L. (2003) Supporting student learning from experience. In H. Fry, S. Ketteridge and S. Marshall (eds), *A Handbook for Teaching and Learning in Higher Education: Enhancing Academic Practice*, 2nd edn. London: Kogan Paul, pp. 134–47.

Biggs, J. and Moore, P. (1993) *The Process of Learning*. Englewood Cliffs, NJ: Prentice-Hall.

Bishop, V. (1994) Clinical supervision for an accountable profession. *Nursing Times*, 90, 39, pp. 35–7.

Boud, D. and Walker, D. (1998) Promoting reflection in professional courses: the challenge of context. *Studies in Higher Education*, 23, 2, pp. 191–206.

Boud, D., Keogh, R. and Walker, D. (1985) *Reflection: Turning Experience into Learning*. London: Kogan Page.

Brashears, F. (1995) Supervision as social work practice: a reconceptualisation. *Social Work*, 40, 5, pp. 692–9.

Braye, S. and Preston-Shoot, M. (1995) *Empowering Practice in Social Care*. Buckingham: Open University Press.

Brown, A. and Bourne, I. (1996) *The Social Work Supervisor*. Buckingham: Open University Press.

Burgess, H. and Jackson, S. (1990) Enquiry and action learning: a new approach to social work education. *Social Work Education*, 9, 3, pp. 3–19.

Byrne, C. (1994) Devising a model health visitor supervision process. *Health Visitor*, 67, 6, pp. 195–8.

Cartney, P. (2000) Adult learning styles: implications for practice teaching in social work. *Social Work Education*, 19, 6, pp. 609–26.

CCETSW (1996) *Assuring Quality in the Diploma in Social Work – Rules and Requirements for the DipSW*, 2nd edn. London: CCETSW.

Clark, C. (2000) *Social Work Ethics: Politics, Principles and Practice*. Basingstoke: Palgrave Macmillan.

Coulshed, V. and Orme, J. (1998) *Social Work Practice: An Introduction*. Basingstoke: Macmillan.

Crawford, K. and Walker, J. (2003) *Social Work and Human Development*. Exeter: Learning Matters.

Cross, V. (1994) From clinical supervisor to clinical educator: too much to ask? *Physiotherapy*, 80, 9, pp. 609–11.

**Dalrymple, J. and Burke, B.** (1995) *Anti-Oppressive Practice: Social Care and the Law*. Buckingham: Open University Press.

**D'Cruz, H. and Jones, M.** (2004) *Social Work Research: Ethical and Political Contexts*. London: Sage.

**Dearing, R.** (1997) *Higher Education in the Learning Society*. London: National Committee of Inquiry into Higher Education.

**Department of Health** (2002) *Requirements for Social Work Training*. London: Department of Health.

**Dewey, J.** (1933) *How We Think*. Boston, MA: D.C. Heath.

**Dewey, J.** (1938) *Logic: The Theory of Inquiry*. Troy, MN: Rinehart & Winston.

**Doel, M. and Shardlow, S.** (1998) *The New Social Work Practice: Exercises and Activities for Training and Developing Social Workers*. Aldershot: Arena.

**Dominelli, L.** (2002) *Anti-Oppressive Social Work Theory and Practice*. Basingstoke: Palgrave Macmillan.

**Ebbutt, D.** (1996) Universities, work-based learning and issues about knowledge. *Research in Post-Compulsory Education*, 1, 3, pp. 357–72.

**Edwards, C.** (2003) The involvement of service users in the assessment of Diploma in Social Work students on practice placements. *Social Work Education*, 22, 4, 341–9.

**Eraut, M.** (1995) Schön shock: a case for reframing reflection in action. *Teachers and Teaching*, 1, 1, pp. 9–22.

**Erwin, T.** (1991) *Assessing Student Learning and Development*. San Francisco: Jossey-Bass.

**Fade, S.** (2004) Reflection and assessment. In S. Tate and M. Sills (eds), *The Development of Critical Reflection in the Health Professions*. London: Higher Education Academy, pp. 96–100.

**Fook, J.** (2002) *Social Work: Critical Theory and Practice*. London: Sage.

**Fook, J., Ryan, M. and Hawkins, L.** (2000) *Professional Expertise: Practice, Theory and Education for Working in Uncertainty*. London: Whiting & Birch.

**Ford, K. and Jones, A.** (1987) *Student Supervision*. London: Macmillan.

**Fowler, J.** (1995) Nurses' perceptions of the elements of good supervision. *Nursing Times*, 91, 22, pp. 33–7.

**Fry, H., Ketteridge, S. and Marshall, S.** (2003) Understanding student learning. In H. Fry, S. Ketteridge, and S. Marshall (eds), *A Handbook for Teaching and Learning in Higher Education: Enhancing Academic Practice*, 2nd edn. London: Kogan Page, pp. 9–25.

**Furniss, J.** (1988) The client speaks again. *Pro-file*, 3, pp. 2–3.

**Gardiner, D.** (1989) *The Anatomy of Supervision*. Milton Keynes: Society for Research into Higher Education/Open University Press.

**Golightley, M.** (2004) *Social Work and Mental Health*. Exeter: Learning Matters.

**Gould, N. and Taylor, I.** (1996) *Reflective Learning for Social Work*. Aldershot: Ashgate.

**Gray, D.** (2001) Work-based learning, action learning and the virtual paradigm. *Journal of Further and Higher Education*, 25, 3, pp. 315–24.

**GSCC** (2002) *Code of Practice for Employers*. London: GSCC.

**Hart, G. and Rotem, A.** (1995) The clinical learning environment: nurses' perceptions of professional development in clinical settings. *Nurse Education Today*, 15, 1, pp. 3–10.

**Hawkins, P. and Shohet, R.** (2000) *Supervision in the Helping Professions: An Individual, Group and Organizational Approach*. Buckingham: Open University Press.

**Hogan, F.** (2002) The creative possibilities of supervision. *Journal of Practice Teaching*, 4, 1, pp. 44–60.

**Honey, P. and Mumford, A.** (1982) *The Manual of Learning Styles*. Maidenhead: Peter Honey.

**Hopkins, G.** (1998a) *Plain English for Social Services: A Guide to Better Communication*. Lyme Regis: Russell House.

**Hopkins, G.** (1998b) *The White Stuff: A Guide to Effective Writing in Social Care and Related Services*. Lyme Regis: Russell House.

**Horne, M.** (1999) *Values in Social Work*, 2nd edn. Aldershot: Ashgate.

**Howe, D.** (ed) (1996) *Attachment and Loss in Child and Family Social Work*. Aldershot: Avebury.

**Humphries, B.** (1998) Adult learning in social work education: towards liberation or domestication. *Critical Social Policy*, 23, pp. 8–21.

**Illeris, K.** (2003) Towards a contemporary and comprehensive theory of learning. *International Journal of Lifelong Education*, 22, 4, pp. 396–406.

**International Association of Schools of Social Work and International Federation of Social Workers** (2001) Joint agreed definition, 27 June 2001. Copenhagen.

**Issitt, M.** (1999) Toward the development of anti-oppressive reflective practice: the challenge for multi-disciplinary working. *Journal of Practice Teaching*, 2, 2, pp. 21–36.

**Ixer, G.** (1999) There's no such thing as reflection. *British Journal of Social Work*, 29, 6, pp. 513–27.

**Ixer, G.** (2003) Developing the relationship between reflective practice and social work values. *Journal of Practice Teaching*, 5, 1, pp. 7–22.

**Johns, C.** (2000) *Becoming a Reflective Practitioner*. Oxford: Blackwell.

**Johns, R.** (2003) *Using the Law in Social Work*. Exeter: Learning Matters.

**Kadushin, A.** (1976) *Supervision in Social Work*. New York: Columbia University Press.

**Kadushin, A.** (1977) *Consultation in Social Work*. New York: Columbia University Press.

**Kearney, P.** (2003) *A Framework for Supporting and Assessing Practice Learning*, SCIE Position Paper No. 2. London: SCIE.

**Kitwood, T.** (1997) *Dementia Reconsidered: The Person Comes First*. Buckingham: Open University Press.

**Knight, J.** (2003) Assessment of fieldwork practice: the student experience. *Journal of Practice Teaching*, 5, 1, pp. 39–60.

**Knowles, M.** (1984) *Andragogy in Action*. San Francisco: Jossey-Bass.

**Knowles, M.** (1990) *The Adult Learner: A Neglected Species*, 4th edn. Houston, TX: Gulf.

**Kolb, D.** (1984) *Experiential Learning*. Englewood Cliffs, NJ: Prentice-Hall.

**Koprowska, J.** (2004) *Interpersonal and Communication Skills in Social Work*. Exeter: Learning Matters.

**Laming, H.** (2003) *The Victoria Climbié Inquiry Report*, Cmnd 5730. London: Stationery Office.

**Ledbetter, A.** (1989) Organising the teaching of practice. In R. Canton (ed), *Learning at Work*, CCETSW Paper 27.1. London: CCETSW.

**Leveridge, M.** (2003) Preparation for practice – developing and assessing DipSW students' pre-placement competence. *Social Work Education*, 22, 3, pp. 321–7.

**Long, A. and Chambers, M.** (1996) Supervision in counselling: a channel for personal and professional change. *Counselling*, 7, 1, pp. 50–4.

**McCormack, B. and Hopkins, E.** (1995) The development of clinical leadership through supported reflective practice. *Journal of Clinical Nursing*, 4, 3, pp. 161–8.

**McDowell, L. and Sambell, K.** (1999) Fitness for purpose in the assessment of learning: students as stakeholders. *Quality in Higher Education*, 5, 2, pp. 107–23.

**Maidment, J.** (2003) Problems experienced by students on field placement: using research findings to inform curriculum design and context. *Australian Social Work*, 56, 1, pp. 50–60.

**Munro, E.** (1998) Improving social workers' knowledge base in child protection work. *British Journal of Social Work*, 28, 1, pp. 89–106.

**Munson, C.** (1981) Style and structure in supervision. *Journal of Education for Social Work*, 17, pp. 65–72.

**Nathan, J.** (2002) The advanced practitioner: beyond reflective practice. *Journal of Practice Teaching*, 4, 2, pp. 59–84.

**Noble, C.** (2001) Researching field practice in social work education: integration of theory and practice through the use of narratives. *Journal of Social Work*, 1, 3, pp. 347–60.

**Parker, J.** (1999) Education and learning for the evaluation of dementia care: the perceptions of social workers in training. *Education and Ageing*, 14, 3, pp. 297–312.

**Parker, J.** (2001) Interrogating person-centred care in social work and social care practice. *Journal of Social Work*, 1, 3, pp. 329–46.

**Parker, J.** (2003) Positive communication with people who have dementia. In T. Adams and J. Manthorpe (eds), *Dementia Care*. London: Arnold, pp. 148–63.

**Parker, J. and Bradley, G.** (2003) *Social Work Practice: Assessment, Planning, Intervention and Review*. Exeter: Learning Matters.

**Pawson, R., Boaz, A., Grayson, L., Long, A. and Barnes, C.** (2003) *Types and Quality of Knowledge in Social Care*. London: SCIE.

**Payne, M.** (1997) *Modern Social Work Theory*, 2nd edn. Basingstoke: Macmillan.

**Preston-Shoot, M. and Agass, D.** (1990) *Making Sense of Social Work: Psychodynamics, Systems and Practice*. Basingstoke: Macmillan.

**Rai, L.** (2004) Exploring literacy in social work education: a social practices approach to student writing. *Social Work Education*, 23, 2, pp. 149–62.

**Ramsden, P.** (2003) *Learning to Teach in Higher Education*, 2nd edn. London: RoutledgeFalmer.

**Randall, P. and Parker, J.** (2000) Communication theory. In M. Davies (ed), *The Encyclopaedia of Social Work*. Oxford: Blackwell, p. 69.

**Rautkis, M. and Koeske, G.** (1994) Maintaining social worker morale: when supportive supervision is not enough. *Administration in Social Work*, 18, 1, pp. 39–60.

**Redman, P.** (2001) *Good Essay Writing: A Social Sciences Guide*, 2nd edn. London: Sage/Open University Press.

**Rogers, C.** (1967) *On Becoming a Person*. London: Constable.

**Sawdon, D.** (1986) *Making Connections in Practice Teaching*. London: NISW.

**Schön, D.** (1983) *The Reflective Practitioner*. London: Temple Smith.

**Schön, D.** (1987) *Educating the Reflective Practitioner*. San Francisco: Jossey-Bass.

**Schön, D.** (2002) From technical rationality to reflection-in-action. In R. Harrison, F. Reeve, A. Hanson and J. Clarke (eds), *Supporting Lifelong Learning. Volume One. Perspectives on Learning*. London: Routledge/Open University Press.

**Shardlow, S.** (2003) A view from 2010: the BSocW, where are we now? *Journal of Practice Teaching*, 4, 3, pp. 68–74.

**Shardlow, S. and Doel, M.** (1996) *Practice Learning and Teaching*. Basingstoke: Macmillan.

**Shulman, L.** (1993) *Interactional Supervision*. Washington, DC: NASW.

**Sibeon, R.** (1990) Comments on the structure and forms of social work knowledge. *Social Work and Social Sciences Review*, 1, 1, pp. 29–44.

**Stoltenberg, C. and Delworth, U.** (1987) *Supervising Counselors and Therapists*. San Francisco: Jossey-Bass.

**Tate, S.** (2004) Using critical reflection as a teaching tool. In S. Tate and M. Sills (eds), *The Development of Critical Reflection in the Health Professions*. London: Higher Education Academy, pp. 8–17.

**Tate, S. and Sills, M.** (eds) (2004) *The Development of Critical Reflection in the Health Professions*. London: Higher Education Academy.

**Taylor, I. and Burgess, H.** (1995) Orientation to self-directed learning: paradox or paradigm. *Studies in Higher Education*, 21, 1, pp. 87–98.

**Thomas, R.** (2002) Creative assessment: involving service users in student assessment in social work. *Social Work Education*, 4, 1, pp. 27–43.

**Thompson, N.** (1997) *Anti-Discriminatory Practice*, 2nd edn. Basingstoke: Macmillan.

**Thompson, N.** (2000) *Theory and Practice in Human Service*. Buckingham: Open University Press.

**Thompson, N.** (2003) *Communication and Language: A Handbook of Theory and Practice*. Basingstoke: Palgrave Macmillan.

**Thompson, N., Osada, M. and Anderson, B.** (1994) *Practice Teaching in Social Work*, 2nd edn. Birmingham: PEPAR.

**TopssEngland** (2003) *National Occupational Standards for Social Work*. http://www.topssengland.net

**Vroom, V. and Deci, E.** (1992) *Management and Motivation*. Selected Readings. London: Penguin.

**Watson, F., Burrows, H. and Player, C.** (2002) *Integrating Theory and Practice in Social Work Education*. London: Jessica Kingsley.

# Index